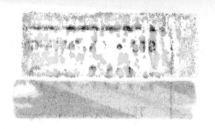

Jacobean Tragedy

Jacobean Tragedy

THE QUEST FOR MORAL ORDER

Irving Ribner

LONDON

Methuen & Co. Ltd

TOTOWA, NEW JERSEY

Rowman and Littlefield

First published 1962
This edition reprinted 1979
by Methuen & Co. Ltd
11 New Fetter Lane, London EC4P 4EE
ISBN 0 416 72500 7

and

Rowman and Littlefield
81 Adams Drive
Totowa, New Jersey 07512
ISBN 0 8476 6179 2

© *The Estate of Irving Ribner 1962*

Printed in Great Britain by
Whitstable Litho Ltd, Whitstable, Kent

British Library Cataloguing in Publication Data

Ribner, Irving
Jacobean tragedy.–(Methuen library reprints).
1. English drama (Tragedy)–History and criticism
2. English drama – 17th century – History and criticism
3. English drama – Early modern and Elizabethan,
1500-1600 – History and criticism
I. Title
822'.051   PR658.T7
ISBN 0-416-72500-7

For only by breasting in full the storm and cloud of life, breasting it and passing through it and above it, can the dramatist who feels the weight of mortal things liberate himself from the pressure, and rise, as we all seek to rise, to content and joy.

MATTHEW ARNOLD

FOR

CLIFFORD AND JONATHAN

Contents

Preface

In *Patterns in Shakespearian Tragedy* I suggested that to be truly great tragedy must spring from the artist's moral concern, his need to come to terms with the fact of evil in the world, and out of his exploration of disaster to arrive at some comprehensive vision of the relation of human suffering to human joy. I suggested also that the great ages of tragedy have been those in which an established system of values was being challenged by a new scepticism, and that Shakespeare was able to effect his tragic reconciliation by affirming in poetic terms the validity of his age's Christian humanism. His tragedies lead to a sense of order, justice and divine purpose in the universe.

I propose in the following pages to explore the manner in which Shakespeare's fellow dramatists, each in his own way, met the same challenge of a growing Jacobean scepticism and disenchantment with traditional values. The writers of tragedy I have chosen to consider are those who I believe most seriously attempted the kind of resolution of the problem of mankind's relation to the forces of evil in the world at which Shakespeare aimed. None succeeded in the same way, but the tragedies they wrote are all conditioned by this quest for moral order, and when they are examined in these terms they reveal new dimensions. This does not imply that they may not be studied with profit in other ways.

Like all who venture to write in this area, I have been profoundly indebted to the late Professor Una M. Ellis-Fermor's *Jacobean Drama*, and the reader will perceive also that I have been strongly influenced by Miss M. C. Bradbrook's *Themes and Conventions of Elizabethan Tragedy* and Professor F. P. Wilson's *Elizabethan and Jacobean*. When my work was in final draft,

The Moral Vision of Jacobean Tragedy by Robert Ornstein was published by the University of Wisconsin Press. Although Professor Ornstein and I approach the subject through different avenues and with different premisses and come usually to quite different conclusions, we are both concerned with the moral value of Jacobean tragedy. I regret that I did not see his work in time to make more use of it, but I have tried to indicate in my notes some of our areas of agreement and, more often, disagreement.

For my references to specific plays it has been difficult to find texts of a uniform reliability. I have been able to use the excellent 'Revels Plays' editions under the general editorship of Professor Clifford Leech for *The Changeling* (ed. N. W. Bawcutt, London, 1958) and *The White Devil* (ed. J. R. Brown, London, 1960). For Middleton's *Women Beware Women* I have used the edition by A. H. Bullen (London, 1885), and for the plays of George Chapman I have relied upon the editions of the late T. M. Parrott (London, 1910 and 1914). For *The Duchess of Malfi* I have modernized the spelling of F. L. Lucas's 1958 edition, based upon his own 1927 monumental edition of Webster's complete plays. For *A Woman Killed With Kindness* I have used the Mermaid edition by A. Wilson Verity (London, 1888), and for *The Rape of Lucrece* I have modernized the edition by Allan Holaday (Urbana, Ill., 1950). For the Cyril Tourneur plays I have modernized the text of Allardyce Nicoll (London, 1929), and for the John Ford plays that of Henry de Vocht (Louvain, 1927). To facilitate reference, I have retained the line numberings of the particular editions I have used. I am grateful to the editors of *ELH*, *Modern Language Review*, *The Tulane Drama Review* and *Tulane Studies in English* for permission to reprint some portions of the book which were printed in more tentative form while the work was in progress.

The earliest portions of this book in time of composition were read to a highly critical group of undergraduates in Miss Enid Welsford's sitting-room in Cambridge in the Spring of 1959. For the comments of all my listeners, and particularly those of Miss Welsford, I have continued to be grateful.

CHAPTER ONE

Introduction

The most important writer of tragedy in the Jacobean era, of course, is William Shakespeare. Not only do such plays as *Othello*, *Lear*, *Macbeth* represent the highest reaches tragedy has attained in any age by the perfection with which they mirror a vision of man's relation to his universe, but the plays of Shakespeare served also as models for his Jacobean contemporaries to emulate. Beaumont and Fletcher, Heywood, Webster and Ford all reveal the influence of their master. But Shakespeare, while he taught his contemporary dramatists much of their craft, is still not one of them. While they imitate his language and ape his situations, the writers of tragedy in the early years of the seventeenth century generally find it difficult to accept without question the view of man's position in the universe which gives to Shakespeare's greatest tragedies their most significant form.

Thomas Heywood is one exception. Conservative like Shakespeare, he continued to espouse throughout his career a view of the universe as the harmonious creation of an ever-loving God, the parts of creation observing order and degree, with every element enjoying its proper function as part of the divine plan. Man was at the centre of the universe, the noblest work of God, his life guided and controlled by the power of divine providence. In such a view of the world evil was real and active, and Heywood like Shakespeare is not afraid to portray its operation, but the means of overcoming evil are always available to man, and although sinners like Macbeth might suffer damnation, the movement of the cosmos was towards a constant rebirth of good out of evil. The end of tragedy written in terms of such a cosmic view was always reconciliation, with the forces of evil at least temporarily vanquished in spite of the horror they have wrought. In *Patterns in Shakespearian Tragedy* I have tried to suggest that Shakespeare's tragedies represent successive attempts to embody in drama steadily more comprehensive visions of the eternal conflict of man against the forces of evil in the world, so as to lead to an affirmation of order and design in the universe, and that they do this in terms of the optimistic Christian humanism of the early Renaissance which stressed always the dignity of man and the providence of God.[1]

But Shakespeare wrote his profoundest plays in an age when their philosophical assumptions already were beginning to appear anachronistic, when Christian humanism was losing its dominance in the more thoughtful minds, and newer, more pessimistic notions of man's position in the universe were gaining supremacy. The seventeenth century is one in which man, as F. P. Wilson has written, 'revised his conception of the external universe and of his relation to it, revised also his conception of himself and of the powers of his mind. . . . Where the emphasis had been upon order and degree, hierarchy and discipline, man's duty to God and the Prince, some now placed it on rights – the rights of the individual conscience, of criticism, of reason.'[2] It is an age out of which finally was to emerge in triumph at the end of the century the new belief in progress and human perfectibility which Francis Bacon had heralded, and it was to be the true beginning of our modern era, but the seventeenth century had to go first through a period of doubt, confusion, and profound pessimism. The Jacobean dramatists do not reflect the new scientific optimism of Bacon, although in Webster's emphasis upon the dignity of human life in spite of the world's corruption there may be some suggestion of what finally is to come. Jacobean tragedy more generally reflects the uncertainty of an age no longer able to

[1] See Herschel Baker, *The Dignity of Man* (Cambridge, Mass., 1947); Douglas Bush, *The Renaissance and English Humanism* (Toronto, 1939); Hardin Craig, *The Enchanted Glass* (New York, 1936); E. M. W. Tillyard, *The Elizabethan World Picture* (London, 1943).

[2] *Seventeenth Century Prose* (Berkeley, Calif., 1960), p. 1. See also Wilson's brilliant analysis of the cleavage between the Elizabethan and Jacobean eras in *Elizabethan and Jacobean* (Oxford, 1945). Perhaps the most comprehensive study of the decline of Christian humanism in the seventeenth century is Herschel Baker, *The Wars of Truth* (Cambridge, Mass., 1952).

believe in the old ideals, searching almost frantically for new ones to replace them, but incapable yet of finding them.

The early seventeenth century is the age of paradox. This is a dominant literary exercise of the time, developed in the best of Jacobean prose, and a cardinal element in its metaphysical poetry. I have already indicated that Shakespeare, in his final tragedies, *Antony and Cleopatra* and *Coriolanus*, when he had thoroughly explored the implications of his own Christian humanism, came at last to a paradox which he could not resolve.[1] These final plays reveal a world in which man may be destroyed by evils which are the inevitable concomitants of those very virtues which make him great, and in which the lust of Antony or the pride of Coriolanus – examples of vice in traditional terms – may have an heroic quality to which we cannot help but give our emotional acquiescence while we recognize the corruption of divine order from which it springs and its utter sinfulness in terms of traditional morality. Shakespeare brought his hero at the end of *Coriolanus* to a point where he could not renounce sin without also renouncing virtue. In these final plays of paradox, and not in the great positive affirmations of *Othello*, *Lear*, and *Macbeth*, Shakespeare reveals his affinity to the Jacobean dramatists who were his fellows and successors.

We are not to assume that the tragedy of the Elizabethan period was universally orthodox in its moral position. There has been intellectual division and dissent in every era in human history, and among the Elizabethan dramatists there was an important tradition of scepticism whose leading exponent was Christopher Marlowe. He had questioned the order and perfection of the universe and the workings of divine providence in all his plays; even in *Dr Faustus*, with its outward framework of religious belief and its morality play technique, Marlowe had protested against a system of values which decreed damnation as the price of knowledge and the power inherent in it. Professor Una M. Ellis-Fermor has indicated the spirit of Marlovian tragedy, with its steadily increasing sense of human limitations and its tone of human defeat, as that which comes to dominate the Jacobean era, and she has seen this 'mood of spiritual despair' as the

[1] *See Patterns in Shakespearian Tragedy* (London, 1960), pp. 168–201.

product of Marlowe's continuing exploration of the political system of Niccolò Machiavelli.[1]

Although Machiavelli had tried to divorce politics from ethics as two separate areas of human concern, he did not entirely succeed in doing so. The inevitable ethical implications of his political creed tended to emphasize a new materialistic view of the universe in direct opposition to the divinely oriented Christian humanism of Richard Hooker and William Shakespeare, and this new materialism, Miss Ellis-Fermor holds, fostered the spiritual uncertainty of Jacobean tragedy. But the emergence of Machiavelli in Italy in the early years of the sixteenth century is merely one evidence of the spirit of scepticism which is as much a part of the Renaissance as its Christian humanism. Bruno and Montaigne exerted a wide influence as well, and the new astronomy in the early seventeenth century was a direct challenge to all which men traditionally had believed about the permanence and immutability of the heavens.

The brief career of Christopher Marlowe may serve as a kind of index to the shifting currents of Renaissance thought. He came up to Cambridge as a Parker Foundation scholar, destined for the Anglican ministry and presumably committed to its doctrinal position which he must have absorbed at the King's School in Canterbury. After his wide reading of theology in the library at Corpus Christi College, he seems to have turned to the new Renaissance scepticism, and in his *Tamburlaine* we find an enthusiastic espousal of the premises of Machiavelli, coupled with an exuberance and faith in the potentialities of mankind. He breathes the spirit of Renaissance vitality and optimism. But in the second part of *Tamburlaine* we find already a painful awareness of the limitations placed upon mankind by the very fact of mortality. As he grows older his disillusion steadily increases until in *Edward II* we find him rejecting his earlier faith in the fall of Mortimer,[2] and if *Dr Faustus* is his final play, as is now generally

---

[1] *The Jacobean Drama* (London, 1936), pp. 1–5. See also Wilson, *Elizabethan and Jacobean*, pp. 100–1; Robert Ornstein, *The Moral Vision of Jacobean Tragedy* (Madison, Wis., 1960), pp. 24–31.

[2] I have dealt with these matters in 'Marlowe and Machiavelli', *Comp. Lit.*, VI (1954), 349–56, and *The English History Play in The Age of Shakespeare* (Princeton, 1957), pp. 127–36.

supposed, it may be also his most pessimistic statement of human limitation and frustration. Marlowe began, in short, embracing the new challenge to the old orthodoxy, and he ended disillusioned with the new but still incapable of accepting the old. He arrived at the spirit of negation and disillusion which is the mark of Jacobean tragedy.

Seventeenth-century literature reflects this lack of spiritual certainty in its concern with death, time, and mutability, and in the pervasive spirit of melancholy already fully drawn in Shakespeare's *Hamlet*, the subject for pseudo-scientific analysis in Burton's *Anatomy*, and surviving in the quiet sadness of Ford's *Broken Heart*. There is a renewed interest in a notion which has its roots in the waning of the Middle Ages, but which in the seventeenth century becomes an important source of controversy and a leading motif in literature: the idea that the world is in its antiquity, nearing the end of a long period of progressive decay which had begun with the fall of man, and rapidly approaching total dissolution. It has been argued that the revival of this belief owed much to the new astronomy.[1] The discovery in 1572 of a new celestial body among the fixed stars led men to question the very notion that there were fixed stars. The heavens no longer appeared to be the immutable evidence of an unchanging, perfectly unified creation, in which the destiny of mankind, past and future, could be read. The continuing discoveries of the astronomers culminated in Galileo's discovery in 1612 of spots in the sun, which seemed to indicate that the heavens themselves were subject to decay. Dr Godfrey Goodman in 1616 proclaimed his thesis of a decaying world in his widely influential *The Fall of Man*, in which he related this decay to the fall of Adam and Eve from Paradise, as Sir Walter Ralegh had related it some two years before in his *History of the World*. Goodman was answered in 1627 by Dr George Hakewill in his finally more important work, *An Apology of the Power and Providence of God in the Government of the World*, which espoused instead the idea of human progress.

[1] George Williamson, 'Mutability, Decay and Seventeenth Century Melancholy,' *ELH*, II (1935), 121–50. See also D. C. Allen, 'The Degeneration of Man and Renaissance Pessimism,' *SP*, XXXV (1938), 202–27; R. F. Jones, *Ancients and Moderns* (St. Louis, Mo., 1936), a condensed version of which appears in *The Seventeenth Century* (Palo Alto, Calif., 1951), pp. 10–40.

Hakewill's position finally was to triumph, but it is not a position which is reflected in the tragedies of the period, for these reflect a search for moral order in a world which seems in its senility, giving constant evidence of death, decay, and eternal change. In this fact Jacobean tragedy is not associated with that movement in seventeenth-century thought which is best represented by Hakewill and Bacon. It is associated rather with the despair for humanity which runs through Ralegh's *History of the World*, the concern with death and decay and the corrosion of time which are constant motifs in the poetry of John Donne, and the melancholy tone of Sir Thomas Browne's *Urn-Burial*, which has aptly been called the age's great funeral sermon for a world in dissolution.

As part of this melancholy vision of human destiny, we find a renewed interest in the ancient notion of the four ages of man, of which every schoolboy read in Ovid's *Metamorphoses*. The present is seen as the 'iron age', and the 'golden age' comes to be identified with the period before the fall of Adam and Eve from Paradise, when the forces making for decay and degeneration had not yet been set in motion. There is a tendency also to look back with nostalgia upon classical antiquity – long accorded a special place by the Renaissance humanists – as a time when the world was inhabited by a nobler race of men, less defiled and vitiated by the process of deterioration. The dominant philosophy of the Jacobean era comes to be one which had emerged in different forms in the most pessimistic times of the ancient world, in the Hellenistic period of Greece and in the Rome of the later emperors. This is the philosophy of stoicism, which was perhaps most influentially proclaimed in the Renaissance by Justus Lipsius in his *De Constantia* of 1583, a work which embraced the theory of the world's deterioration and offered as the only means of survival in such a world a stoic control of human emotions and a consequent imperviousness to pain, with an awareness that the destruction of the world was part of the inevitable scheme of things. This work was translated into English by John Stradling. It went through several editions and was widely influential in disseminating the ideas both of the degeneration of the world and of how man might live in spite of it.

These notions are reflected with a particular clarity in the tragedies of George Chapman. His *Bussy D'Ambois*, as I shall try to show in the following chapter, is based upon the assumption of a degenerate decaying world in which virtue is incapable of survival. To make his point Chapman uses the concept of the 'golden age' of prelapsarian perfection, for Bussy reflects the qualities of man in such an age, and his tragedy is the tragedy of all of us who must live in a world where such virtues can no longer exist. These motifs are repeated in the *Byron* plays, with further emphasis upon the corroding force of the world's evil, and with a slowly developing stoic insistence on the need for authority to regulate a degenerate humanity. In *The Revenge of Bussy D'Ambois* and *Caesar and Pompey* Chapman sacrifices everything else in the plays to his need to proclaim, almost frantically, the virtues of the stoic ideal. There is little stoicism in his final play, *The Tragedy of Chabot*, but his theme is the inability of justice to survive in a vitiated world, and the mood is that of the early *Bussy D'Ambois*.

Chapman's career as a writer of tragedy may illustrate that drive which produced also the greatest plays of the other dramatists with whom the following chapters will be concerned. It is a drive to find a basis for morality in a world in which the traditional bases no longer seem to have validity. The greatest tragedians of the Jacobean era seek in their various ways to discover some meaning in human suffering, some kind of affirmation which can make life possible in a world which seems to give reason only for despair. This quest, I believe, has been the traditional mission of tragedy as an art form, and it is the goal which Shakespeare in his way most triumphantly achieved. The dramatists we are here considering all seek ways of their own, and although none is so successful as Shakespeare, in the moral earnestness of their striving, and in the poetic imagination with which they reflect the tensions of their world, we have what gives to their works their distinctive character.

D. C. Allen has written that whereas human suffering in the Middle Ages could be accepted as the road to heaven, the Jacobean era could look upon it with no such certainty, and he has attributed the pessimism of the age to the failure of Renaissance

philosophers to create out of conflicting modes of thought a
synthesis as satisfying as that which Aquinas had shaped for
their medieval forebears.[1] This failure of synthesis is what ties the
Jacobean era to our own and gives to its literature so much imme-
diacy. It is a failure, we must not forget, which has not been
without its compensations, for it has made possible the idea of progress and enlarged the possibility of scientific advance and a perhaps
someday to be hoped for amelioration of the human condition.

Far as the seventeenth century may be from the Middle Ages
in this respect, the writers of the Jacobean period tend to fall back
upon motifs particularly characteristic of the medieval mentality.
Of this fact the two plays attributed to Cyril Tourneur may offer
most striking evidence. Here we have all the symbols traditionally
associated with medieval asceticism; the human skull, the charnel
house, the seven deadly sins paraded across the stage, the bitter
excoriations of lust and gluttony, and a world whose evils are
drawn with such brutal exaggeration that they would be merely
ludicrous could we not see them in terms of medieval *contemptus
mundi* as the author's way of arguing that man must place his
hopes in the world to come.

Tourneur is unique in his age for the moral fervour with which
he uses the drama to espouse a primitive Christianity more closely
related to that of the medieval world than to that of the seventeenth century. It is not, however, a philosophy entirely of escape
from the evils of the world, for implicit in it, as I shall try to show,
is the means of overcoming these evils. Tourneur employs the
weapons developed by medieval and Renaissance satirists, but his
final goal is something more than a plea for social improvement;
it is a larger vision of man's relation to the cosmos. His Christianity is of another sort than that of Thomas Heywood, with his
faith in the essential goodness of man and in the power of love
and divine providence to overcome the evils of the present world.
Tourneur's Christianity is based upon the assumption of a decaying universe and a corrupt and degenerate humanity. His primary
concern is the salvation of the soul, as that part of man which can
survive and transcend the chaos of the world. Heywood also, as
A Woman Killed with Kindness may superbly illustrate, is com-

[1] *SP*, XXXV (1938), 202–27.

mitted to the Christian thesis that the soul's fate must be man's most significant concern.

Generally, the Jacobean dramatists are firmly Christian in their orientation, although their Christianity may take different forms, as we may see by a comparison of Heywood with Tourneur. In some dramatists such as Chapman, Christian belief receives so little emphasis that the possibility of human salvation is virtually excluded from the moral framework of their plays. This is true also of John Webster who, while he refers constantly to heaven and hell in conventional terms and fills his plays with commonplaces of Christian sentiment, nevertheless creates a world which is incompatible with any system of religious belief. Webster is nevertheless among the dramatists who succeed most notably in their search for moral order. He bases this order not upon divine influence in human affairs, but in a celebration of the dignity of human life which renders man superior to his world, and he finds his basis for morality in the need to preserve this dignity which separates man from beast at any cost, for it is man's only weapon against the chaos of the world. In this attitude Webster is related to that current of his age which points out of Jacobean uncertainty and despair towards the future, for it was in terms of man's human strength and initiative that men like Francis Bacon sought to resolve their age's dilemma.

Thomas Middleton, on the other hand, is as fully Christian in his orientation as Heywood or Tourneur. His moral categories are clear and precise. There is never any question of the reality of evil or of its absolute distinction from good. Nor is there any doubt of the punishment the sinner must suffer inevitably in a world governed by an inexorable force of divine retribution. But Middleton's is neither the optimistic religion of Heywood nor the heaven-oriented Christianity of Tourneur. His vision is one of hell and damnation. His world is gloomier far than that of Webster, for he offers little hope for human triumph. There is, as I shall suggest, a Calvinistic strain in Middleton which grows more and more marked as we move from *The Changeling* to *Women Beware Women*. In both plays he is concerned with the revelation of an evil which man is incapable of escaping. His constant theme is man's slow awareness of his own damnation, which he is able to portray with a psychological realism unique in his age. In *Women Beware Women* we seem to have a symbolic vision of the damnation of all mankind.

The final dramatist with whom we will be concerned is John Ford. His literary career begins near the end of the Jacobean period, and his great tragedies all belong to the age of King Charles. But Ford looks back as surely as any of his contemporaries to the great Elizabethans for his inspiration, and among his plays the echoes of Shakespeare's language are perhaps most frequent. In Ford we find a melancholy nostalgia for the Elizabethan age which he imitates but of which he never can be a part. His tragedies reveal an acute awareness that the world of Shakespeare is no more, and this awareness lends the characteristic note of sadness to his plays. Ford reflects both the scepticism of his own age and a longing for the kind of ordered moral universe which this scepticism rejects. His tragic heroes stand literally between two worlds, the one dead and the other incapable of being born, and his tragic vision is a view of mankind incapable of achieving the kind of moral order without which survival is impossible. Ford's moral earnestness has not been sufficiently recognized by his critics, although they have usually pointed to the negation which is the only resolution of which he is capable.

The dramatists we are considering express their visions of man's relation to his universe in different ways. Of primary importance in all of them is the shaping of a particular story so that its parts, in the usual manner of myth, will combine to give expression to a moral statement, and so that particular characters may stand for particular moral positions, and in their conflict with one another opposing moral commitments be resolved. Some rely upon specific moral preachment. Tourneur's *Atheist's Tragedy* carries this method to an extreme, and this is one reason why this play is so much inferior to *The Revenger's Tragedy*, where the moral substance of the play is more perfectly conveyed in the total dramatic structure. Tourneur relies heavily upon his poetic imagery to emphasize his themes and to establish the tone of his plays, as does Webster in both of his Italian tragedies and Middleton in *Women Beware Women*, although *The Changeling*, a far greater play in most respects, is comparatively weak in this. Heywood and

Ford are barren in poetic imagery when compared to Webster or Tourneur. Chapman shapes his total play as a reflection of a specific philosophical point of view. To this end, even in his most successful plays, he sacrifices consistency of character and plot, and he does not hesitate to insert long speeches of didactic commentary to further his philosophical argument at the price of his dramatic structure. His diction is complex and involuted, and he packs his poetry with constantly recurring symbols, those of the tree and the ship at sea being two of his favourites. These occur in different contexts in almost every one of his plays. I propose in the following chapters to examine the moral vision of six dramatists by means of a close analysis of selected plays, and each play will be approached according to the particular technique upon which the individual dramatists most heavily depend.

In spite of their diversity of technique, what all of these writers of tragedy have in common is that their moral purposes are controlling factors in their plays, shaping character, plot and poetry so as to give expression to the presiding moral statement. This is generally true of Elizabethan and Jacobean tragedy. Only in Shakespeare, and occasionally in a dramatist like Middleton or Webster, is a moral vision expressed in terms of characters who have much resemblance to men and women we might have known or in situations which are likely to have occurred.[1] I shall stress in the following chapters, as I stressed in *Patterns in Shakespearian Tragedy*, the conventional, symbolic dimension of the Jacobean stage, with its roots in the medieval drama, and its constant use, in the medieval manner, of the specific symbol to express the universal truth. I will suggest that these dramatists, like Shakespeare, are always more interested in mankind than in individual men, and that they rarely hesitate to sacrifice the consistency of character portraiture to the needs of the larger symbolic statement which is the play as a whole. We cannot hope to understand the horrors of Tourneur or Webster while we try to see their plays as realistic accounts of events which might have occurred, and forget that the painted skull at the lecher's lips was a traditional symbol with connotations deeply rooted in medieval iconography.

---

[1] Wilson, *Elizabethan and Jacobean*, pp. 100–8, has stressed this point, as has M. C. Bradbrook, *Themes and Conventions of Elizabethan Tragedy* (Cambridge, 1935).

I have been able to analyse in the following chapters only a handful of the tragedies of the Jacobean era. There are some powerful and important products of multiple authorship, such for instance as *The Witch of Edmonton*, to which I have paid no regard, largely because such works tend to reflect a vision which is unlike that of any of the individual contributing authors, and it is upon the total attitudes and developments of individual dramatists that I wish to place my emphasis. There are also some dramatists of towering importance in their time whose works I have not chosen to dwell upon. It is impossible to overestimate the influence of men like Marston, Jonson, Beaumont and Fletcher. I do not believe, however, that any of the dramatists I am excluding from full consideration ever succeeded in conveying a total vision of the relation of mankind to the forces of evil in the universe; the impulse behind their tragedies was smaller and generally directed towards immediate social rather than larger cosmic issues. Those dramatists upon whom I am concentrating my attention all reflect a total – and therefore a truly moral – vision of the destiny of mankind, and this vision they are capable of conveying with the truth inherent in the greatest of poetry. Thomas Heywood admittedly never reaches the heights attained by the others, but I have included him as the dramatist who most perfectly illustrates the survival of a conservative tradition against which the greater plays of his contemporaries may be measured. If *The Rape of Lucrece* is a bad play, it is nevertheless a sincere attempt to express a view of mankind which we cannot ignore if we are to have any true understanding of the Jacobean age.

John Marston is in many ways a greater dramatist than Heywood, and he certainly left a heritage which his contemporaries more assiduously imitated. It could be argued, in fact, that next to Shakespeare Marston is the most influential dramatist of his age. In his plays we find the devices which are to be used with greater artistry by Webster, Tourneur, Middleton and Ford. The hero of the atrocious *Antonio's Revenge* shows his influence in Tourneur's Vindice, and we probably could not have had Webster's Bosola and Flamineo without the example of Marston's Malevole. Marston created the pattern for the malcontent; he developed the Machiavellian villain, and he is Kyd's great successor in revenge tragedy.

He showed his followers how to end a play in the bloody holo-caust of a final masque scene. He is a master of dramatic irony, and the technique of *The Malcontent*, with its central omnipotent char-acter manipulating the action, is reflected in later plays of such diversity as *The Revenger's Tragedy*, *Measure for Measure*, and *The Tempest*.

Yet Marston, in spite of his influence on others, wrote no play himself which is truly significant among the tragedies of his age. This is true in spite of the indignant, crusading spirit which marks everything he wrote. Marston succeeds only in being moralistic, never in attaining the truly moral vision. This is so because his impulse is essentially satiric rather than tragic. He is concerned with attacking vice, painting it in its most horrible and revolting forms. He is not concerned with the relation of good and evil to one another within the cosmos, or with the relation of human suffering to human joy. He is incapable of that kind of acceptance of the fact of evil which is implicit in any total cosmic vision. Behind his plays is always the impulse to destroy evil by revealing how horrible or ludicrous it truly is, and thus his end is not the understanding of the human condition, but rather the improve-ment of social life by the eradication of vice. In this distinction is much of the difference between tragedy and satire.

Antonio's Revenge and *The Insatiate Countess*, while they deal with suffering and death, and in spite of the greatness of much of their poetry, are rendered absurd by Marston's satiric impulse. The only one of his plays which really can be called a tragedy is that neglected play he wrote at the end of his literary career, before he abandoned the stage and disappeared into the obscurity of the church. This play is *Sophonisba, or The Wonder of Women*, which T. S. Eliot in a rather surprising reversal of the usual judgment, has called the greatest of Marston's works.[1] But the very qualities which lead Eliot to praise this play are, I believe, what render it also so unlike the plays with which we are here concerned. *Sophonisba* does not seem to spring from any attempt to reconcile the confusion and uncertainties of the Jacobean age; it springs rather from Marston's admiration for the ancients, for it is above all else an exercise in Senecan imitation. Eliot is perceptive in

1 *Selected Essays* (London, 1951), pp. 230-3.

pointing to the greatness of much of its poetry, but the play's moral statement is little more than the typical Senecan acknowledgment of the supremacy of fate and the need for man to face his destiny with stoical courage and acceptance. It reflects the moral dilemma of Marston's age only to the extent that it illustrates that tendency to look to the classical world for models of an excellence which men in the degenerate present may strive to emulate, and it is similar to Chapman's *Caesar and Pompey*. It does not reflect that agonized struggle with the realities of the dramatist's own age which marks Chapman's greater and more successful plays. Eliot writes that one must come to this play fresh from Corneille and Racine, that it belongs with the French and English classicists rather than with the Shakespearians. This fact sets it apart from that current in Jacobean tragedy with which we are concerned.

What is true of *Sophonisba* is in large measure true also of Ben Jonson's two Roman tragedies, for they also are the products of classical imitation, the only essays in tragedy of a dramatist whose greatness lay in other areas. Not the tragic but the satiric spirit is the key to Jonson's greatness, and it is why he achieved his stature as one of the greatest writers of English comedy. He knew how to attack the evils of mankind, and he did so effectively in comedy, his goal being always the satirist's object of social improvement. His conception of the goals of tragedy is clearly outlined in the address to the readers which he prefaced to the 1605 edition of *Sejanus*, where he listed among its essential qualities, 'truth of argument, dignity of persons, gravity and height of elocution, fullness and frequency of sentence'. In these principles Jonson is following not his own native dramatic tradition, but the neo-classical critics of France and Italy, Scaliger and Castelvetro. All of the qualities he lists are evident in his *Sejanus* and *Catiline*, but these remain among the last read of all his plays. They do not reveal the kind of struggle for a vision of man's role in the universe which is an essential feature of the greatest tragedies. Jonson's Roman plays belong, perhaps, more closely in the tradition of Roman satire than they do in that of English tragedy.

Sejanus and *Catiline* remain the scholar's attempts to achieve a classical ideal in tragedy, and like Marston's plays they are moralistic rather than moral, for they do not use the events of Rome to reflect, as Shakespeare always does in his Roman tragedies, upon the larger questions of mankind in general. Roman history is used for the parallels it may afford to the specific political vices of Jonson's own day. His supposed tragedies reveal the same impulse towards social correction which more properly governs Jonson's comedies. He is concerned not with mankind but with the corruption in the court of King James. His 'fullness and frequency of sentence' becomes not a statement of general moral truth, but simply the repetition of commonplace moral injunctions gleaned from the ancients, and primarily from Seneca. His 'truth of argument' gives to his plays perhaps a greater validity as history than as tragedy, while his 'dignity of persons' and 'gravity and height of elocution' firmly link his plays to the Senecan ideal he is imitating, with its heavy reliance upon essentially sterile devices of rhetoric. *Sejanus* and *Catiline* in many respects are interesting plays, and they deserve perhaps a greater place than usually has been accorded to them in critical estimates of Jonson's achievement, but they do not belong in the company with which we here are concerned.

The final years of the Jacobean era are dominated by the influence of Beaumont and Fletcher, through the plays they wrote individually and together, and through those which they produced in collaboration with Massinger, Field and Shirley. Their influence is strong upon John Ford, and I shall suggest that only as he learned to overcome this influence did Ford write the kind of truly moral tragedy which links him rather with Shakespeare and Webster. Although the tragedies of Beaumont and Fletcher are concerned with ethical and political problems, and although their work is an intimate reflection of the age which produced it, the kind of tragedy they wrote – of which *The Maid's Tragedy* is the finest example – is incapable of expressing the kind of moral vision with which we are concerned.

J. F. Danby has pointed to Beaumont and Fletcher as the dramatists who best express a nostalgia for Elizabethan values – the elegant aristocratic life of the great house – which can no longer survive in the seventeenth century, and he has called *The Maid's Tragedy* a perfect reflection of the tensions of the

Jacobean world.[1] There is much truth in this, and it is possible to see Aspatia, as Danby sees her, as a symbol of the rejected Elizabethan values, and Amintor as the symbol of an honour which consists only in outward appearance, and thus is only a debased shadow of the true code of honour represented by Melantius. Beaumont and Fletcher might have written truly moral tragedy. I would suggest that they failed to do so because of their very attachment to a past social ideal which may never have fully existed except in men's minds, and because the ethical paradoxes they examine are related only to artificial – and ultimately unimportant – patterns of social conduct, and never to the larger problem of the relation of good to evil in the world. There is, moreover, no real working through of these paradoxes in their plays, no evidence of real intellectual and emotional involvement, what Eliot has called a struggle for harmony in the soul of the poet. The paradoxes which form the central conflicts of their plays are resolved by dramaturgy, the clever manipulation of situation, with a masterly control of shock and suspense. There is no real quest for moral certainty in their plays, only the facile reduction of artificially contrived paradoxes, with no attempt to resolve moral issues.

The Maid's Tragedy rings its many changes on the themes of honour, love and friendship, values dear to the Elizabethan world of Wilton and Penshurst, but in this play reduced to a specious shallowness. Amintor is torn at first between his love for Aspatia and his loyalty to the king, two conflicting absolute values, and we must remember that Beaumont and Fletcher are as conservative as Heywood in their doctrine that the king, no matter how evil he may be, must be unconditionally obeyed. Amintor must sacrifice the honour of his betrothed for his loyalty to the king. When he learns that Evadne is the king's whore, he is again torn between duty and honour, for he cannot oppose the king who has made him a cuckold. The shallowness of the ideal of honour to which these characters so thoroughly are committed is revealed by Evadne: she has married Amintor to preserve an honour which in truth already has been forfeited, and to do so she must destroy the honour of her husband by making him a cuckold. In the same

[1] *Poets on Fortune's Hill* (London, 1952), pp. 152–206.

way Amintor must be a knowing bawd to his wife in order to preserve his own honour because to reveal his cuckoldry is to destroy his reputation and thus his honour. Honour here is a meaningless pretence.

Similarly, Melantius, when Amintor calls Evadne a whore, must kill his friend to preserve the non-existent honour of his sister. When Melantius, moved by friendship, finally offers to kill the king to preserve the honour of Amintor, his friend draws his sword against him, for an exposure of the king again will destroy Amintor's reputation. Melantius is faced with the paradox that to preserve the already forfeited honour of his family he must destroy the already forfeited honour of his friend.

Such paradoxes have no validity in moral terms because they are merely explorations of the nuances of a code of behaviour which has no relation to reality, and it is a code from which no character is capable of the slightest departure. Their absolute stances represent no real moral positions, merely varieties of pretence. The paradoxes must be resolved if the audience is to be satisfied, and for this purpose Beaumont and Fletcher use the simple device of having Evadne undergo a sudden reformation and then murder the king. The conflict of absolutes upon which the play is constructed is in no way resolved. No moral statement emerges, although in the death of Aspatia there may be, as Danby holds, a lament for the beauties of a world which can be no more.

The great popularity of such drama may signal the decline of tragedy of real moral intensity. In the plays of Beaumont and Fletcher we see the triumph of theatricality over philosophical substance. This may be related to the growing dominance of the particular coterie theatre for which these dramatists wrote, the influence of the court with its particular tastes and attitudes, and the gradual relegation of the great popular theatre for which Shakespeare wrote to the confines of the lower middle class audiences at the Red Bull.

It is also true that in the age of Shirley and Massinger many of the intellectual conflicts of the Jacobean era were ceasing to have the intensity they had had when Chapman, Tourneur and Webster were writing their plays. The great issues of the seventeenth century were approaching some resolution. The idea of human progress had begun to triumph; the new scientific age was coming into its maturity, and England was becoming more deeply involved in the political and social problems which in 1642 were to bring the theatres to a close. The plays of Massinger and Shirley are no longer vehicles for profound self discovery and philosophical statement. They are exploitations for the sake of an amusement-loving court of the theatricality learned from Beaumont and Fletcher. A play like Shirley's *The Cardinal*, although brilliantly constructed and no doubt extremely effective upon the stage, is merely the shallow imitation of only some external features of Webster's Italian tragedies. These men succeed most notably in facile court comedy. The great age of English tragedy had come to a close with John Ford, some ten years before the closing of the theatres.

CHAPTER TWO

George Chapman

I

We are not sure when in the long career of George Chapman, spanning the last decades of Elizabeth's reign and all of that of James, he turned to the writing of tragedies, but the earliest of them could not have been written much later than 1603, when a new king ascended the English throne and a new era began. It would be fitting indeed if *Bussy D'Ambois* could be dated with certainty in that year,[1] for Chapman's first tragedy is a mirror of the pessimism which comes to dominate the vision of the Jacobean era, and his later plays reveal his attempts to resolve moral conflicts which are particularly a part of that era. He comes to do so in terms of a stoic philosophy learned from classical antiquity. *The Revenge of Bussy D'Ambois* and *Caesar and Pompey* are his most deliberate efforts to teach his age such a stoic creed; that they are the least successful of his plays may stem in part from Chapman's own inability to embrace wholeheartedly the philosophy he proposed. It is very significant that in his *Tragedy of Chabot*, first written probably in 1614 at the end of his career as a dramatist, and years later revised in collaboration with the younger James Shirley, Chapman seems to renounce the stoicism he had espoused in the intervening plays and to reassert the moral vision of his early *Bussy D'Ambois*. Chapman's career as a writer of tragedy reflects that search for moral order out of which the greatest of Jacobean tragedies emerged, but Chapman's search led to no such affirmation as we shall note particularly in the plays of Tourneur and Webster. It led to failure and resignation.

All great tragedy has its didactic and allegorical dimension, for

[1] It has been dated as early as 1597. On the chronology see Elias Schwartz, 'The Dates and Order of Chapman's Tragedies,' *MP*, LVII (1959), 80–82. The most comprehensive study of Chapman is Jean Jacquot, *George Chapman* (1559–1643): *sa vie, sa poésie, son théâtre, sa pensée* (Paris, 1951).

it succeeds only to the extent that out of it emerges some general view of man's relation to his world, a view which transcends the immediate fate of the particular characters with whom the play is concerned. Tragedy must move always from the specific to the general. In the greatest tragedians, like Shakespeare and Webster, the didactic function is subsumed into the total structure of the play. In Chapman it is not. He is the most deliberately didactic tragedian of his age. He wrote to Sir Thomas Howard in his dedication to *The Revenge of Bussy D'Ambois* of 'material instruction, elegant and sententious excitation to virtue, and deflection from her contrary, being the soul, limbs, and limits of an authentical tragedy'. To this end Chapman sacrificed all else. It has been pointed out that after *Bussy D'Ambois* his development was not towards a fusion of his poetic talents with the needs of the drama, but rather towards an exclusion from his plays of every element of drama which did not further his ethical purpose.[1]

Chapman proudly proclaimed as the function of the artist what others more diffidently accomplished: he sought to teach his age how to live. Although we recognize Chapman's avowed didacticism, however, we must avoid the temptation to reduce his plays to moral *exempla*, as some critics have done, or to consider the total body of Chapman's work as the reflection of an ethical system which the poet had fully evolved before he began to write and of which the various poems and plays merely reflect different aspects.[2] Chapman's tragedies, as I have suggested, fall into at least three major divisions, reflecting different stages in his intellectual growth. His career like that of almost every major writer was one of constant development and change.[3]

---

[1] See Moody E. Prior, *The Language of Tragedy* (New York, 1947), p. 111.

[2] These dangers are reflected in Ennis Rees, *The Tragedies of George Chapman: Renaissance Ethics in Action* (Cambridge, Mass., 1954), a study which has done much to redirect our attention to Chapman's moral content. On its limitations, see also Robert Ornstein, *The Moral Vision of Jacobean Tragedy*, pp. 48 ff.

[3] On Chapman's changing perspective in tragedy, see the essays by Elias Schwartz: 'Seneca, Homer, and Chapman's *Bussy D'Ambois*,' *JEGP*, LVI (1957), 163–76; 'Chapman's Renaissance Man: Byron reconsidered,' *JEGP*, LVIII (1959), 613–26. Ornstein sees Chapman's career as one of steady progression from the supposed moral confusion of *Bussy D'Ambois* to the stoicism of *Caesar and Pompey* which he takes to be Chapman's latest and most mature intellectually play, one which seems 'to complete the pattern of his tragedies and to represent the end of a long artistic and intellectual pilgrimage' (p. 79).

Chapman's greatest achievement in tragedy is the play with which he began, *Bussy D'Ambois*. It is not – as it traditionally has been regarded – Chapman's celebration of the self-sufficient 'complete man' whose own *virtù* places him above morality and whose stoic fortitude makes him the master of his world.[1] But neither is the play a work of orthodox Christian humanism, as Rees maintains, which holds up the fate of Bussy, one of Chapman's 'bestial servants of self love', as a 'cautionary example' of what might happen to any man who allowed his passion to govern him, challenged the just laws of society, and permitted lust to overcome his reason and render him its slave. We cannot approach this play in the simple terms of whether Chapman approved or disapproved of Bussy, for this is greatly to oversimplify the author's complex tragic vision.

I would suggest that Bussy D'Ambois is deliberately shaped as a dramatic symbol of humanity, faced with a problem which all mankind must face. In this we have much of the difference between moral *exemplum* and the kind of philosophical exploration which is tragedy. It is this range which links Chapman to Shakespeare. In *Bussy D'Ambois* Chapman set himself to answer in drama the ancient question of how man, endowed by his creator with reason, strength and knowledge of virtue, can live in a world corrupted by evil. But to this question Chapman can find no answer, and the total impact of his play, conveyed with a striking emotional force, is to affirm that virtue cannot survive, for it must inevitably be corrupted and destroyed by the baseness of the world in which it is forced to live.

In *The Conspiracy of Charles, Duke of Byron*, and its companion *Tragedy of Charles, Duke of Byron*, Chapman returned to the same

---

[1] See, for instance, Parrott, *Tragedies*, pp. 545–6; A. S. Ferguson, 'The Plays of George Chapman,' *MLR*, XIII (1918), 1–24; XV (1920), 223–39. This view is implicit among more recent studies in Michael Higgins, 'The Development of the "Senecal Man": Chapman's *Bussy D'Ambois* and some Precursors,' *RES*, XXIII (1947) 24–33; W. G. McCollom, 'The Tragic Hero and Chapman's *Bussy D'Ambois*,' *Univ. of Toronto Quart.*, XVIII (1949), 227–33; Clifford Leech, '*The Atheist's Tragedy* as a Dramatic Comment on Chapman's *Bussy* plays,' *JEGP*, LIII (1953), 525–30. On Chapman's stoicism, see J. W. Wieler, *George Chapman – The Effect of Stoicism on his Tragedies* (New York, 1949). Wieler, pp. 21–51, finds little stoic philosophy in *Bussy D'Ambois*. I would agree with Ornstein (p. 51), that Bussy is 'an isolated virtuous man without a place in the society which destroys him', but I cannot agree that the total play is confused in its moral point of view.

theme, but these plays do not extend the moral vision of *Bussy D'Ambois*, although certain elements receive greater emphasis. Byron at the beginning of his career is as heroic as Bussy in his assertion of the rights of the natural man, but he is even more blackened by sin than Bussy at its close, with the virtuous king Henry IV, against whom he conspires, to emphasize the complete degeneration which Byron has undergone, and to suggest, as Chapman had not suggested before, the need for human authority in spite of the world's evils. Elias Schwartz[1] has seen in the *Byron* plays a transition between *Bussy D'Ambois* and *The Revenge of Bussy*, the two opposite poles of Chapman's vision. In Chapman's ambivalence towards Byron – an admiration for his heroic stature which persists even while he most strongly condemns him for his behaviour – Schwartz sees a movement towards a new ethical outlook.

There is truth in this, but the transition involves no changing view of the world or of man's position in it. The world of Bussy is the world of Byron, and it is still the world of Clermont D'Ambois. But in Clermont Chapman tried to create a man who by practising a kind of virtue could survive in spite of the world, as Bussy and Byron could not. That Clermont is never more than a wooden figure, his behaviour as absurd as it is essentially inconsistent, and that *The Revenge of Bussy D'Ambois* is entirely incapable of imparting the emotional impact in which the truth of tragedy must be conveyed, shows the failure of Chapman truly to embody any such moral vision in drama. In *Caesar and Pompey* he tried again, offering the stoic, Cato, as a model for his audience, but this play becomes a series of dull moralistic speeches, entirely ineffective as drama. Only in *Chabot*, at the end of his career, did Chapman again succeed in imparting the emotional equivalent of a moral vision. This play, along with the *Byron* plays and *Bussy D'Ambois*, must represent the essence of Chapman's contribution to English tragedy. I should like here to concentrate upon *Bussy D'Ambois* and *Chabot*, the plays which mark the beginning and the end of Chapman's writing of tragedy, and in which his moral vision is most perfectly expressed.

[1] *JEGP*, LVIII (1959), 613–26.

II

Critics traditionally have pointed to Chapman's weakness in character portrayal, and they have compared him unfavourably to Shakespeare in this respect.[1] Such a comparison does grave injustice to Chapman, for it slights the particular quality of his own dramatic artistry. Chapman was not a naturalistic dramatist. He was never concerned with portraiture of character as a significant end in itself. The wide division among critics of *Bussy D'Ambois* may come in part from a failure to recognize that none of the characters in this play was designed as a realistic portrait from life, but that each performs various thematic functions within the total design, and that these functions are often incompatible with one another in terms of psychological verisimilitude. All together they constitute the ethical statement which is the primary concern of the play.[2] Bussy, Monsieur, Tamyra, and the rest may at times be used to comment with the voice of Chapman on the events of the play in terms inconsistent psychologically with the moral positions for which they already have been made to stand. What results is a sometimes confused and always difficult play, more gratifying perhaps to the reader in his study than it has ever been to an audience in the theatre. Part of this difficulty may have resulted from Chapman's failure adequately to work his philosophical substance into the total structure of his play, his tendency to present it in set speeches which themselves are highly poetic, but which are not well integrated into the dramatic action. Chapman, in short, found it difficult to adapt his concept of the dramatist's high philosophical mission to the requirements of a popular stage.

Bussy himself performs three distinct roles within the play. On one level he is a symbol of ordinary humanity, with its mixture of good and evil, striving to live virtuously, but by his very involvement in living inevitably corrupted and destroyed. Man cannot divorce himself, Chapman is saying, from the corrupt

[1] Chapman's ability as a dramatist, however, has been defended by James Smith, 'George Chapman,' *Scrutiny*, III (1934–5), 339–50; IV (1935–6), 45–61.
[2] Some such multiple use of character has been perceived in Chapman's *Byron* plays by Peter Ure, 'The Main Outline of Chapman's Byron,' *SP*, XLVII (1950), 568–88.

society of which he is a part, and as he lives in society man must inevitably be infused with its own corruption until his world destroys him. Chapman's 'nature' is the vitiated and corrupt 'nature' of Renaissance pessimism. For the evil world into which man is born, Chapman probably could find no symbol more meaningful to his audience than that of the corrupt court of Henry III. Bussy's life journey is framed to mirror the awful paradox that to live is to know evil and to die. In his continuing effort to resolve this paradox, Chapman came in later years to create the mythical brother of Bussy, Clermont D'Ambois, who in *The Revenge of Bussy D'Ambois* offers one possible answer: that man may become impervious to the evil of the world and the master of his own fate by the cultivation of his own knowledge and religion and by attuning his human will to the will of God with a confidence in the goodness and wisdom of the divine master plan. There is no such answer in *Bussy D'Ambois*. There is only the heroic spectacle of suffering man at least able to accept his end with courage and fortitude.

On another level Bussy is used to suggest a reason for this tragedy which Chapman sees as the universal lot of man. This reason is the fall of man from Paradise and the consequent corruption of nature which in a large area of Renaissance belief had brought to an end the 'golden age' when man could live by his own natural instincts, sharing in the perfect harmony of God's creation. Then all hierarchies of order and degree, all institutions of government and law were unnecessary. Bussy is framed as a natural man such as lived in this 'golden age'; his own natural instincts are above human laws:

> since I am free,
> (Offending no just law), let no law make
> By any wrong it does, my life her slave:
> When I am wrong'd, and that law fails to right me,
> Let me be king myself (as man was made),
> And do a justice that exceeds the law;
> If my wrong pass the power of single valour
> To right and expiate; then be you my king,
> And do a right, exceeding law and nature:
> Who to himself is law, no law doth need,

Offends no law, and is a king indeed.

(II, i, 194–204)

Bussy is thus described by King Henry III, speaking as choral commentator:

> A man so good, that only would uphold
> Man in his native noblesse, from whose fall
> All our dissensions rise; that in himself
> (Without the outward patches of our frailty,
> Riches and honour) knows he comprehends
> Worth with the greatest: Kings had never borne
> Such boundless empire over other men,
> Had all maintain'd the spirit and state of D'Ambois;
> Nor had the full impartial hand of Nature
> That all things gave in her original,
> Without these definite terms of Mine and Thine,
> Been turn'd unjustly to the hand of Fortune,
> Had all preserv'd her in her prime, like D'Ambois;
> No envy, no disjunction had dissolv'd,
> Or pluck'd one stick out of the golden faggot
> In which the world of Saturn bound our lives,
> Had all been held together with the nerves,
> The genius, and th'ingenuous soul of D'Ambois.

(III, ii, 90–107)

Had D'Ambois, the natural man, prevailed, he is saying, there would be no need for laws, no social ills or inequalities, none of those attributes of a fallen social order which medieval and Renaissance churchmen held to have proceeded from the fall of man from Paradise. That this was a notion close to Chapman's heart we can tell from a passage in *The Gentleman Usher*, which was entered in the Stationers' Register in November, 1605, and thus must have been written close in time to *Bussy D'Ambois*. Here the virtuous Strozza, who through his faith in God has been endowed with a miraculous power of prophecy and wisdom, speaks similar words:

> Had all been virtuous men,
> There never had been prince upon the earth,
> And so no subject; all men had been princes:
> A virtuous man is subject to no prince,
> But to his soul and honour, which are laws

> That carry fire and sword within themselves,
> Never corrupted, never out of rule.
>
> (V, iv, 56–62)

But there are no such virtuous men: the 'golden age' is no more. The tragedy of Bussy is that natural man cannot survive and retain his virtue in the corrupt present world as he might have had not man fallen. Human laws are necessary, as Chapman is to affirm in the magnanimous and pious King Henry IV of the later *Byron* plays, but that these laws are now reflected in the shallow and treacherous Henry III and his brother heightens the tragic irony of Bussy's fall for his unwillingness to recognize their necessity. How Chapman intended us to regard his hero is indicated by the ghost of the Friar:

> Farewell, brave relics of a complete man,
> Look up and see thy spirit made a star;
> Join flames with Hercules, and when thou sett'st
> Thy radiant forehead in the firmament,
> Make the vast crystal crack with thy receipt;
> Spread to a world of fire, and the aged sky
> Cheer with new sparks of old humanity.
>
> (V, iv, 147–53)

This is not the death of the bestial sinner without learning or religion, which Rees sees in Bussy, but of 'old humanity' who cannot survive on earth but will lend splendour to the heavens. This is Chapman's lament that such a man as Bussy D'Ambois can be no more. That the fate of Bussy reflects the general corruption of nature is made clear in an important speech of foreshadowing by Monsieur, speaking here not in his role of villainous plotter, but in that of choral commentator upon the action of the play:

> If thou outlive me, as I know thou must,
> Or else hath Nature no proportion'd end
> To her great labours; she hath breathed a mind
> Into thy entrails, of desert to swell
> Into another great Augustus Caesar,
> Organs and faculties fitted to her greatness;
> And should that perish like a common spirit,
> Nature's a courtier and regards no merit.
>
> (IV, i, 101–8)

This heroic, complete Bussy D'Ambois will not outlive the vile
politician, Monsieur. He will die like a common creature, and in
this defeat Chapman mirrors the corruption of nature which has
lost forever the harmonious perfection of the 'golden age' before
the fall.

With these two functions of Bussy, as symbol of ordinary man
and as symbol of prelapsarian perfection, is combined a third:
that of choral commentator which Bussy shares with most of the
other characters of the play. It is in this role that we find him in
his opening speech, commenting upon the corrupt world he is
about to enter, but of whose corruption we have little reason to
believe he yet has had experience:

> Fortune, not Reason, rules the state of things,
> Reward goes backwards, Honour on his head;
> Who is not poor, is monstrous; only Need
> Gives form and worth to every human seed.
> As cedars beaten with continual storms
> So great men flourish . . .
> Man is a torch borne in the wind; a dream
> But of a shadow, summ'd with all his substance.
>
> (I, i, 1–19)

In this imperfect world, where greatness is an illusion, and where
a capricious fortune (the very first word of the play) rules the
lives of men, there is only one resort:

> We must to virtue for her guide resort,
> Or we shall shipwreck in our safest port.
>
> (I, i, 32–33)

On another level the speech introduces us to Bussy, the young
man about to enter the world. His poverty – Chapman's quite
unhistorical innovation – is symbol both of his virtue and of that
alienation from the world of men which in a corrupt society must
be the price of virtue. He 'neglects the light and loves obscure
abodes' (I, i, 47), but this is a role foreign to the nature of man,
and when Monsieur comes to offer him wealth and position, he
cannot refuse this symbol of entry into the active world, although
he knows the shallowness of the world he enters and that he will
be but a pawn in the hands of the power-hungry Monsieur. He

accepts the decree of fortune that man must assume the social role of man, but he trusts in his own virtue to protect him:

> He'll put his plow into me, plow me up;
> But his unsweating thrift is policy,
> And learning-hating policy is ignorant
> To fit his seed-land soil; a smooth plain ground
> Will never nourish any politic seed;
> I am for honest actions not for great;
> If I may bring up a new fashion,
> And rise in Court for virtue, speed his plow!
>
> (I, i, 123-30)

Before the end of the play Bussy will have himself embraced the 'policy' he now decries in Monsieur; his initial virtue will not save him. He knows the world into which he enters, but he rationalizes his choice:

> Man's first hour's rise is first step to his fall.
> I'll venture that; men that fall low must die,
> As well as men cast headlong from the sky.
>
> (I, i, 141-3)

No sooner has Bussy's choice been made than Chapman shows with a fine dramatic irony that Bussy's virtue will be to no avail. His first fruit of his new social role is gold, and in receiving this he must cope with human avarice, embodied in the loathsome and obsequious Maffé. Thus Bussy begins his first quarrel, and thus he acquires the first of the enemies who will at last destroy him. The French court is all affectation and pretence, and when Bussy enters it he must assume the normal role of the courtier which is reflected in his formal and artificial wooing of the Duchess of Guise. Bussy, the natural man, however, will not accept the social canons of order and degree, and his baiting of his superior, the Duke of Guise, wins him another more powerful enemy. In the contrapuntal lines of Bussy's wooing of the duchess and baiting of her husband we have the two roles of Bussy neatly juxtaposed: ordinary man entering the corrupt world and assuming its values, and the natural man rebelling against the false values of that very world.

From the false code of courtly dalliance Chapman turns to the false code of courtly honour, by whose rules also man in society must live. Thus Bussy must fight with the taunting nobles, Barrisor, L'Anou and Pyrot, and the result must be the death of five men, including the great soldier of France and the two friends, Brisac and Melynell, who have come to Bussy's aid. This in terms of the world's law is murder, as King Henry declares (II, i, 149), but Monsieur, in a choral role, defends the action as the proper behaviour of the natural man:

> Manly slaughter
> Should never bear the account of wilful murther,
> It being a spice of justice, where with life
> Offending past law equal life is laid
> In equal balance, to scourge that offence
> By law of reputation, which to men
> Exceeds all positive law, and what that leaves
> To true men's valours (not prefixing rights
> Of satisfaction, suited to their wrongs)
> A free man's eminence may supply and take.
>
> (II, i, 150–159)

But no man in the corrupt present world can be truly free. Bussy's very exercise of the attributes of the natural man has made him a murderer in terms of the world's law, just as it will make him an adulterer.

The relation between Bussy and Tamyra has been described as one of passionate lust. What is remarkable, however, is that Chapman, who knew well how to paint the lust of Monsieur and the jealous frenzy of Montsurry, does not dwell at all on any lustful passion on Bussy's part. The lust of Monsieur, Chapman's own addition to the historical story, serves rather to set off by contrast the utterly different love of Bussy for his lady. She is an embodiment of the animal passion which is a part of the nature with which Bussy must live. He is introduced to Tamyra by the Friar as one fitting to satisfy the passion of a noble lady:

> Come, worthiest son, I am past measure glad,
> That you (whose worth I have approv'd so long)
> Should be the object of her fearful love;
> Since both your wit and spirit can adapt
> Their full force to supply her utmost weakness:
> You know her worths and virtues, for report
> Of all that know is to a man a knowledge:

> You know, besides, that our affections storm,
> Rais'd in our blood, no reason can reform.
> Though she seek then their satisfaction
> (Which she must needs, or rest unsatisfied)
> Your judgment will esteem her place thus wrought,
> Nothing less dear than if yourself had sought.
>
> (II, ii, 133–45)

In responding to Tamyra Bussy is accepting the normal condition of corrupted nature over which human reason can have no control. He has not sought her love, but in the world he has entered the role of the illicit lover is a natural one, and he assumes it as lightly as he had assumed the defence of his honour against his sneering detractors. That adultery is the normal way of the French court had been made clear by Monsieur in pressing his own suit of Tamyra:

> Honour, what's that? Your second maidenhead:
> And what is that? A word: the word is gone,
> The thing remains: the rose is pluck'd, the stalk
> Abides; an easy loss where no lack's found:
> Believe it, there's as small lack in the loss
> As there is pain i'the losing; archers ever
> Have two strings to a bow; and shall great Cupid
> (Archer of archers both in men and women)
> Be worse provided than a common archer?
> A husband and a friend all wise wives have.
>
> (II, ii, 10–19)

Even Montsurry counsels his wife to bear the advances of Monsieur, since immorality is the prerogative of princes (II, ii, 68–84).

That Bussy should begin his intrigue with Tamyra is thus, on the one hand, the inevitable result of his entry into the world and his acceptance of its values, and on the other an ordinary exercise of the functions of natural man. Their love is dictated by necessity,[1] as Tamyra affirms for the audience:

[1] See Hardin Craig, 'Ethics in Jacobean Drama: The Case of Chapman,' in *The Parrott Presentation Volume* (Princeton, 1935), pp. 25–46. The important role of fortune or necessity in the play has been recognized also by Smith, *Scrutiny*, IV (1935–6), 50, who writes that 'in the matter of vice, both she [Tamyra] and the whole of mankind are at the mercy of nature'. This emphasis in the play makes it impossible for us to view Bussy, like Rees, as a 'cautionary example'. Nature being what it is, his fate cannot be escaped..

> It is not I, but urgent destiny,
> That (as great statesmen for their general and
> In politic justice, make poor men offend)
> Enforceth my offence to make it just.
> What shall weak dames do, when the whole work of nature
> Hath a strong finger in each one of us.
>
> (III, i, 62–67)

The theme of an invidious fortune guiding Bussy's life is worked into the texture of the play.

Tamyra, whose inconsistency has so puzzled critics of the play, is cast by Chapman as a symbol both of the natural force which man cannot evade and of the conflict between the demands of this force and those of the social order. Her frenzied protestations first of loyalty to her husband, then of passion for Bussy and of shameful remorse for her transgressions, are reflections of this conflict for which she stands. Bussy, in his role as natural man, can feel none of this conflict. His relation to Tamyra is the natural relation of man and woman belonging to a 'golden age' without the restraints of marriage (symbolized by the union of Tamyra and Montsurry which can evoke no real feeling other than that of the wronged husband who must defend his honour at whatever human cost). Bussy loves outside all moral law; he has no sense of sin:

> Sin is a coward, madam, and insults
> But on our weakness, in his truest valour:
> And so our ignorance tames us, that we let
> His shadows fright us.
>
> (III, i, 20–23)

The affair between Bussy and Tamyra is the crucial element in his career and the immediate cause of his death. It is, on the one hand, a dramatic reflection of the involvement in sin which is the inevitable consequence of living, and on the other it is the free expression of the normal qualities of natural man and woman. These two motifs are fused, for the burden of the drama is that natural man cannot survive in a corrupt world. A treacherous servant must reveal the lovers' secret; the jealous frustration of Monsieur must vent itself in a drive for the most inhuman retribution, and the demands of society's code of honour must provoke the injured husband to a vehement animal fury, reflected in the stabbing of Tamyra and her torture upon the rack: 'the course I must run for mine honour's sake' (V, i, 25), as her husband explains it.

The summoning of the spirits, Behemoth and Cartophylax, at the end of the fourth act provided the Jacobean audience with the kind of sensationalism it relished, and we must not forget that Chapman, in spite of his philosophical bent and of the strong vein of poetic symbolism in his plays, knew well how to please the cruder tastes of his audience. But this episode serves other functions as well. With the knowledge of the plot against him which the spirits provide, Bussy is able to embrace his end knowingly and bravely and by his last heroic gestures affirm the dignity of man in spite of the world's evil which he has come to share. By providing Bussy with this knowledge Chapman is able also to illuminate another facet of his hero's corruption; Bussy now vows to meet his enemies with that very 'policy' which has been the mark of Monsieur, and to which at the beginning of the play Bussy had been so strongly opposed:

> I'll soothe his plots, and strow my hate with smiles,
> Till all at once the close mines of my heart
> Rise at full date, and rush into his blood:
> I'll bind his arm in silk, and rub his flesh,
> To make the vein swell, that his soul may gush
> Into some kennel where it longs to lie,
> And policy shall be flank'd with policy.
> Yet shall the feeling centre where we meet
> Groan with the weight of my approaching feet:
> I'll make th'inspired thresholds of his court
> Sweat with the weather of my horrid steps,
> Before I enter, yet will I appear
> Like calm security before a ruin:
> A politician must like lightning melt
> The very marrow, and not taint the skin:
> His ways must not be seen; the superficies
> Of the green centre must not taste his feet:
> When hell is plow'd up with his wounding tracts:
> And all his harvest reap'd by hellish facts.
>
> (IV, ii, 175–93)

Bussy has accepted the values of Monsieur. He is at the end the corrupt anti-social force which Ennis Rees describes, but what Rees ignores is that this has been a gradual corruption from an initial virtue, that it has been the inevitable result of an involvement in living which no man can evade, and that in the larger symbolism of the play it reflects the general fate of man. Bussy is never the 'cautionary example' which the audience can hold up to scorn and in whose end it can feel the execution of poetic justice. Bussy is a figure with whom the audience must instinctively sympathize, for he stands also for the dignity of man which he upholds to the very end and in which it is the audience's profoundest urge to believe. In Chapman's careful delineation of Bussy as the natural man, moreover, the audience is directed not so much to an awareness of his own sin as to a sense of the corruption of the society which must destroy him. In lamenting the fall of Bussy we lament also the fall of man, and this is a tragic emotion such as an audience can never feel in witnessing the simple punishment of an ignorant sinner.

The Guise and Monsieur, who throughout the play have served as symbols of a corrupt society while also serving as choral commentators, in the fifth act are described as ministers of fate (V, iii, 63–64). They stand now for the necessity which will destroy Bussy, and in a short but significant choral scene they also show the audience how it must regard the ensuing death of the hero. Bussy's nobility and grandeur are affirmed, but such greatness nature must destroy just as it destroys less perfect men:

> Now shall we see that Nature hath no end
> In her great works responsive to their worths.
>
> (V, ii, 1–2)
>
> .   .   .   .   .   .
>   here will be one
> Young, learned, valiant, virtuous, and full mann'd;
> One on whom Nature spent so rich a hand
> That with an ominous eye she wept to see
> So much consum'd her virtuous treasury
> Yet as the winds sing through a hollow tree
> And (since it lets them pass through) let it stand;
> But a tree solid (since it gives no way
> To their wild rage) they rend up by the root:
> So this whole man

> (That will not wind with every crooked way,
> Trod by the servile world) shall reel and fall
> Before the frantic puffs of blind-born chance
> That pipes through empty men, and makes them dance.
>
> (32–45)

Here is no spectacle of just retribution for sin within a Christian moral order. Bussy's death will reflect rather the inevitable end of man at the hands of a vitiated nature which pays no regard to the magnificent traits with which she created him. This common fate of man Bussy can only accept with a heroism fitting his nobility. He goes bravely to his death, sparing the life of Mont-surry in an act of magnanimity, and when he has been treacher-ously shot from behind, speaking chorally for Chapman on the meaning of his life and death:

> 'tis enough for me
> That Guise and Monsieur, Death and Destiny,
> Come behind D'Ambois. Is my body, then,
> But penetrable flesh? And must my mind
> Follow my blood? Can my divine part add
> No aid to the earthly in extremity?
> Then these divines are but for form, not fact:
> Man is of two sweet courtly friends compact,
> A mistress and a servant: let my death
> Define life nothing but a courtier's breath.
>
> (V, iv, 76–85)

The 'two sweet courtly friends' are, as Parrott points out (p. 560), the body and soul of man who are related to one another as the lover to his mistress. It is the tragedy of human life that man's immortal parts cannot preserve his mortal. This fact Bussy accepts, and he will put his faith in the soul which remains:

> I'll not complain to earth yet, but to heaven,
> And, like a man, look upwards even in death.
>
> (V, iv, 88–89)

He celebrates the immortality of his fame and he offers his fate as a symbol of the universal human frailty, in lines which Chap-man translated loosely from the *Hercules Oetaeus* of Seneca:

> Oh my fame,
> Live in despite of murther. Take thy wings

And haste thee where the grey ey'd Morn perfumes
Her rosy chariot with Sabaean spices!
Fly, where the Evening from the Iberian vales
Takes on her swarthy shoulders Hecate
Crowned with a grove of oaks; fly where men feel
The burning axletree, and those that suffer
Beneath the chariot of the snowy Bear:
And tell them all that D'Ambois is hasting
To the eternal dwellers; that a thunder
Of all their sighs together (for their frailties
Beheld in me) may quit my worthless fall
With a fit volley for my funeral.

(V, iv, 98–111)

The frailties of mankind, past and present, are beheld in him. The audience leaves the theatre with a sense of the heroic magnificence of the natural man, and at the same time with a renewed awareness of the common plight of humanity in a world in which this magnificence cannot survive, in which even man's immortal parts cannot preserve him from the evil of a corrupted nature in which he is destined to live. It is to this sombre view of human life that Chapman designed *Bussy D'Ambois* to give poetic expression.

III

That *The Tragedy of Chabot, Admiral of France* has been among the most neglected of Chapman's plays may derive in part from the vein of historical allegory in the play and the consequent tendency of critics to regard its characters merely as transparent masks for specific personalities in the court of King James with no larger significance, and generally to dismiss the play as a propagandistic attempt by an aging dramatist to curry favour for his imprisoned patron. The name of James Shirley which appeared with Chapman's upon the title page of the 1639 quarto has further led most commentators to place it outside the main stream of Chapman's work. I would suggest, however, that in this play Chapman attains an emotional intensity through which he is able to transmit a vision of man's relation to his universe in a manner that is equalled in no other of his later tragedies.

That Chabot represents Robert Carr, Earl of Somerset; that

Poyet stands for Sir Francis Bacon; and that the play represents their separate trials before the courts of James I, has been accepted generally since the notion was first proposed in 1928.[1] It has been agreed also that Shirley merely revised an existing play by the elder dramatist and did little to change its basic form and content. The allegorical reading raises questions, moreover, which cannot be answered within the allegorical framework. If the play holds up Chabot, as most commentators maintain, as an exemplary portrait of the truly virtuous man and in this way argues for the exoneration of the Somerset he represents, how are we to explain the death of Chabot? Both Jacquot and Rees are disturbed by this, and following Mrs Solve, they try to explain it as Chapman's suggestion that if King James does not pardon Somerset he will die of a broken heart like Chabot. But Chabot dies after he has been fully exonerated by King Francis and restored to all of his former dignities. A strict allegorical reading would suggest Chapman's argument that Somerset would die if pardoned. A real allegorist would have had Chabot live, as Somerset actually lived, several years longer than Chapman himself.

The death of Chabot suggests that the design of the tragedy – which derives not from contemporary events, but from Etienne Pasquier's *Les Recherches de la France* (1607, 1611, and 1621) – was conceived without regard to the affairs of Somerset or Bacon and probably is anterior to them, the contemporary allegorical significance having been added in a later revision which did not alter the play's basic structure. I would reconstruct the history of *Chabot* in somewhat the following fashion: the play probably was written first in 1614, at the very end of the period when Chapman was writing for the stage and was most concerned with French history. It was based upon the 1611 edition of Pasquier, where the trials of Chabot and Poyet are presented in the same relation to one

[1] Norma Dobie Solve, *Stuart Politics in Chapman's Tragedy of Chabot* (Ann Arbor, Mich., 1928). Mrs Solve further identified Montmorency as George Villiers, Duke of Buckingham, and the Proctor-General as Sir Edward Coke. Parrott endorsed these views in *JEGP*, XXIX (1930), 300–4. More recent critics are in accord, and of these only Wieler and Ornstein (pp. 76–79) are willing to examine the play independently of the historical allegory. For Ornstein *Chabot* is concerned with the conflict between law and royal prerogative with the absolutism of King James I reflected in Chapman's King Francis and Chabot representing the kind of medieval view of the supremacy of law associated with the position of Coke.

another as in Chapman's play. The work may never have been staged, for the relation of ruler to subject was dangerous matter for the stage, and Chapman had already been in difficulty over the *Byron* plays and his share in *Eastward Ho*. At this time, immediately after the loss of his patron, Prince Henry, the dramatist could ill afford further risks.

As Parrott suggests (p. 633), Chapman probably handed the play to the Queen's Revels company then under the management of his friend, Nathan Field. When this company joined with Princess Elizabeth's Men in 1613, the playbook went with it. Some time after 1621, Shirley, a member of Princess Elizabeth's Men, probably decided to revise Chapman's old play because of its topicality, and Chapman, who had not written a play in a decade, joined with him in revamping the play so that it might reflect more closely upon the Somerset affair, but in no way changing the basic tragic design. Most of the revision must have been by Chapman himself, for Parrott's careful evaluation of their respective shares in the final product shows that Shirley must have been responsible only for toning down some of Chapman's sententious speeches, adding a feminine interest in the relations between the Queen and Chabot's wife, and making the dialogue more natural. Parrott concludes (p. 633) that 'the original design and groundwork of the play as it now stands is Chapman's'. But these are matters about which we never can know anything with real certainty. The important fact is that *Chabot* is a complex and interesting play, and we will have no adequate understanding of the tragic vision it unfolds while we limit our reading of it by what relevance it may have had to the immediate affairs of King James and his court.

The moralist Pasquier had indicated the two lessons to be gleaned from his brief account: (1) that a judge must always base his actions upon principles of justice and not upon the passions or desires of the king who appointed him, and (2) that a great lord who falls into disfavour with his king should, if possible, avoid being tried in a court of justice, for then his least faults will be magnified into the most monstrous crimes. Both of these precepts are carried into Chapman's play. The first is stated by King Francis:

                         of me learning
This one more lesson out of the events
Of these affairs now past: that whatsoever
Charge or commission judges have from us,
They ever make their aim ingenuous justice,
Not partial for reward or swelling favour;
To which if your king steer you, spare to obey,
For when his troubled blood is clear and calm,
He will repent that he pursued his rage,
Before his pious law, and hold that judge
Unworthy of his place that lets his censure
Float in the waves of an imagined favour:
This shipwrecks in the haven, and but wounds
Their consciences that soothe the soon-ebb'd humours
Of their incensed king.

                                    (IV, i, 440–54)

I would suggest, however, that the second lesson may have had an even greater share in shaping Chapman's tragic vision,[1] for implicit in it is the notion of the imperfection of a human justice dependent upon a king. Chapman's play is concerned with this imperfection and the human frailty from which it stems.

The theme of human frailty is introduced in the first scene when Allegre speaks of those qualities in men

        That which in Nature hath excuse, and in
        Themselves is privileg'd by name of frailty.

                                  (I, i, 27–28)

---

[1] This latter moral is ignored by most critics. For Rees (p. 157) the play is a simple account of 'a just man destroyed by unjust treatment, as an appeal to deal mercifully with Somerset'. Rees wisely recognizes that Chapman is 'primarily concerned with universal moral significance' (p. 158), and he seeks to determine how Chapman's play goes beyond the contemporary significance of Somerset's fall, but what moral statement is there in the view of a completely just and good man who suffers momentarily through the evil of others, but who is then entirely vindicated and restored to his former station, only to die of a broken heart? Rees does not answer the crucial question of what in the total tragic design makes it necessary that Chabot die after his virtue has been vindicated so thoroughly. Ornstein (p. 79) sees it as evidence of Chapman's melancholy. Wieler's notion (pp. 117–35) that the play celebrates the triumph of justice and the 'Senecal Man', with Chabot as a mirror of the stoic ideal of justice, suffers from the same weakness, for stoics are not often crushed by temporary reversals of fortune, and they do not commonly die of broken hearts. Wieler's reading of the play leads him, as it inevitably must, to the conclusion that *Chabot* is not a tragedy at all: 'The death of a stoic protagonist simply affirms a devotion to ethical motives in which tragic meaning is never present' (p. 133).

In defending Chabot's devotion to justice, Allegre stresses the admiral's fear that this weakness which man derives from nature should ever guide his actions:

> For, as a fever held him, he will shake
> When he is signing any thing of weight,
> Lest human frailty should misguide his justice.
>
> (I, i, 55-57)

Chabot's death is not a triumph of justice. It is Chapman's tragic acknowledgment of that 'frail condition of strength, valour, virtue' which an earlier Bussy D'Ambois had lamented in his own demise (V, iv, 141). Chabot will learn through his bitter experience

> how vain is too much faith
> And flattery of yourself, as if your breast
> Were proof against all invasions; 'tis so slight,
> You see, it lets in death.
>
> (IV, i, 215-8)

Chabot would live by a principle of perfect, unwavering justice. His tragedy is also his education, for he comes to learn that such an ideal is impossible in an imperfect world. Human justice, Chapman is saying, can only reflect the justice of the cosmos, and this has been corrupted by the fall of man.

There are fewer characters in *Chabot* than in any of Chapman's other plays, and although these may have been revised to resemble figures in the court of James, they were shaped primarily as symbols of various moral positions. The world in which they move is the chance-ridden, transitory world of *Bussy D'Ambois*, where true greatness is an illusion, for the powerful of one day may be the fallen of another, and all are subservient to the power of the king whose whim or passion may control the destiny of men. To be virtuous is to earn the hatred of society, as Allegre also makes clear at the beginning:

> ask a ground or reason
> Of men bred in this vile, degenerate age!
> The most men are not good, and it agrees not
> With impious natures to allow what's honest;
> 'Tis an offence enough to be exalted

> To regal favours; great men are not safe
> In their own vice where good men by the hand
> Of kings are planted to survey their workings.
>
> (I, i, 15–22)

Allegre's function is to comment on the action of the play, as well as by his physical suffering to parallel the mental anguish of Chabot. To make clear the nature of the world in which his hero will fall, Chapman also introduces the father of Chabot's wife. He scorns the world, as Chabot explains to the king:

> because the extreme of height
> Makes a man less seem to the imperfect eye
> Then he is truly, his acts envied more;
> And though he nothing cares for seeming, so
> His being just stand firm 'twixt heaven and him,
> Yet since in his soul's jealousy he fears
> That he himself advanc'd would under-value
> Men plac'd beneath him and their business with him
> Since height of place oft dazzles height of judgment,
> He takes his top-sail down in such rough storms,
> And apts his sails to airs more temperate.
>
> (I, i, 141–51)

The imagery of the ship at sea, subject to the chance of winds and waves, runs through the play, emphasizing the frailty of the human condition, at the mercy always of fortune and an imperfect world. The old man affirms that to be great and to be just at the same time is impossible. Through him Chapman is saying that to be truly just one must retire from the world and not presume to greatness or the power to judge others. The king is always the symbol of human justice, and in a corrupted world the king will be swayed by passions which negate justice at its very source. But man cannot retire from the world like Chabot's father-in-law. He must live in society no matter how corrupt, and it is in his very nature to strive for high place. His involvement in living must be an involvement in sin. Chabot, Montmorency and Poyet represent three different moral positions which man may take in a corrupt world.

Poyet is the man of policy, the object of Chapman's hatred and scorn throughout his career as a dramatist. Poyet willingly embraces the corruption of society and uses this very evil as his means to advancement. He denies all the altruistic emotions of man. Friendship is merely 'fashionable and privileged policy' (I, i, 166). It is

> but a visor, beneath which
> A wise man laughs to see whole families
> Ruin'd, upon whose miserable pile
> He mounts to glory.
>
> (I, i, 234–7)

He stands for the complete negation of justice. The courts can never be more than the instruments of a pernicious royal will, and the art of the advocate is to give to injustice the seeming mask of its opposite. He speaks with the voice of the Machiavel:

> even in nature
> A man is *animal politicum*;
> So that when he informs his actions simply,
> He does it both gainst policy and nature.
>
> (I, i, 184–7)

But his most complete perversion of justice in the fall of Chabot is no more than an execution of the will of the king.

There is some ambiguity in the portrait of Montmorency, perhaps because the original character was expanded and developed to correspond to the actual George Villiers whom Chapman could not afford to offend. He probably had a smaller role in the earlier version of the play. He seems to have been conceived to stand for a *via media* between Chabot and Poyet. He has all of the virtues and the vices of ordinary man, and he fully accepts his role in the social order. He is reluctant to use base means against his rival, for he has a sense of justice:

> In seeking this way to confirm myself
> I undermine the columns that support
> My hopeful, glorious fortune, and at once
> Provoke the tempest, though did drown my envy.
> With what assurance shall the King expect
> My faith to him that break it for another.
>
> (I, i, 206–11)

The image of the tempest links his human frailty to that of the

other characters. Behind his sense of justice is his concern for
his own fortunes, and when he is convinced that he must break
faith in order to advance in the world, he does so, but not without
reluctance:

> Misery
> Of rising statesmen! I must on; I see
> That gainst the politic and privileg'd fashion
> All justice tastes but affectation.
>
> (I, i, 238–41)

Montmorency is a creature of the world whose injustice and
treachery he accepts. He becomes a vacillating figure, moving
from one side to the other, until he comes finally to plead for
Chabot whom he has helped to ruin. He is not committed to evil
like Poyet: 'Good man he would be, would the bad not spoil him'
(II, ii, 27), but his striving after high place corrupts him as
inevitably it must corrupt any man. If there is some inconsistency
in his characterization, this may be the fault of the historical
allegory super-imposed upon it. There is little warrant for his role
in Pasquier.

Chabot cannot learn to live with the world's evil like Montmorency. He is committed to a code of unwavering and exact
justice. He prides himself upon his ability to overcome his human
frailty and to mete out perfect justice, looking to his own innocence to shield him from a hostile world:

> I walk no desert, yet go arm'd with that
> That would give wildest beasts instinct to rescue
> Rather then offer any force to hurt me –
> My innocence, which is a conquering justice
> And wears a shield that both defends and fights.
>
> (II, ii, 53–57)

But no man is truly innocent, for to live is to share in the general
corruption of mankind, and Chabot's fall is Chapman's ironic
commentary upon the power of such belief in innocence to
preserve him.

There is a paradox in Chabot which is similar to that which
Shakespeare had posed in *Coriolanus*. There the hero by unswerving
devotion to the aristocratic ideal comes to deny his kinship to his

fellow men and thus his own nature as a human child of God, falling through his pursuit of an absolute virtue into the sin of pride. Chabot, in the same manner, by his pursuit of an absolute justice, must deny those qualities of human frailty which are the property of fallen man and which make perfect justice impossible. Chabot's very devotion to justice becomes the source of pride, and it is also a source of delusion, for it leads him to place his faith in those human instruments of justice whose lamentable imperfection his tragedy will reveal.

Both the pride and the delusion of Chabot are implicit in his first conflict with the king over his destruction of Montmorency's 'unlawful' bill.[1] The king maintains that he alone has raised Chabot to his position of wealth and power; Chabot argues that his own virtue has made him what he is, and that God will maintain him in his high station even if the king will not:

> But, if the innocence and right that rais'd me
> And means for mine, can find no friend hereafter
> Of Him that ever lives, and ever seconds
> All king's just bounties with defence and refuge
> In just men's races, let my fabric ruin,
> My stock want sap, my branches by the root
> Be torn to death, and swept with whirlwinds out.
>
> (II, iii, 29–35)

This is foreshadowing of Chabot's end, for his final knowledge that his supposed innocence cannot protect him, that the king's whim may have power to destroy him, for 'A great man, I see, may be / As soon dispatch'd as a common subject' (IV, i, 80–81) will kill in him the will to live. Chapman then will use this very symbol of the tree to remind the audience that the fate which Chabot here thinks impossible has in fact come upon him.

What Chabot cannot yet perceive is that his very worldly station is a reflection of the pervasive injustice of the natural order, for it was a commonplace of medieval and Renaissance theologians that all human inequality, the very existence of kingship

---

[1] The legal merits of the case at issue are presented in so ambiguous a fashion that the audience is left with some doubts as to the absolute justice of Chabot's point of view (I, ii, 124–45). Whether or not the French merchant was justified in seizing the Spanish ship might well be debated. Chapman might easily have chosen a more clear-cut example of injustice had he wished to avoid all ambiguity.

and degree became necessary only after the fall of man, and that these reflected the disharmony into which the entire universe then was thrown, a concept, as we have noted, which runs through *Bussy D'Ambois*. No man, the king believes, can achieve riches and power and remain free from worldly taint:

> And who sees you not in the broad highway,
> The common dust up in your own eyes beating,
> In quest of riches, honours, offices,
> As heartily in show as most believe?
> And he that can use actions with the vulgar,
> Must needs embrace the same effects, and cannot (inform him)
> Whatsoever he pretends, use them with such
> Free equity, as fits one just and real,
> Even in the eyes of men, nor stand in all parts
> So truly circular, so sound, and solid,
> But have his swellings-out, his cracks and crannies;
> And therefore, in this, reason, before law
> Take you to her, lest you affect and flatter
> Yourself with mad opinions.
>
> (II, iii, 129–42)

Chabot, the king is saying, cannot escape that sinfulness which is a part of his very being as a man. His very insistence upon his unsullied virtue is a challenge to the king's authority, who asks that Poyet by finding Chabot guilty free him 'from forth a subject's fetters, / The worst of servitudes' (II, iii, 186–7). If man can be as virtuous as Chabot claims to be, the necessity for kingship disappears. This very challenge to the king's authority makes necessary Chabot's destruction. His affirmation of complete innocence is a denial of the fall of man, and thus of the necessity of kingship and of all human institutions which proceed from kingship, including the courts of law themselves. This is the paradox of Chabot's moral position. There can be no doubt, of course, of his innocence of crime in terms of the world's morality, but he lacks the virtue of humility, and out of his very freedom from guilt springs the pride which must destroy him. At the end of the play Chabot will learn a new humility. He will recognize the king's authority as the source of all worldly station, place his faith in mercy rather than justice, and plead for the exoneration of Poyet.

Chabot's trial is a monstrous travesty of justice in which Chapman uses all his powers of ridicule, centring upon the irrelevant garrulity and pomposity of the Proctor-General, who even as early as 1614 might have been modelled after the hated Sir Edward Coke. The lack of evidence against Chabot is patently obvious. The judges are forced to condemn him against their own wills by the threat of the king's displeasure, reminding the audience again that the final executor of the law is always the king.

Chabot enters his ordeal firm in his faith in the king's justice. On this he stakes his life:

> No more; the King is just; and by exposing
> Me to this trial, means to render me
> More happy to his subjects and himself.
> His sacred will be obey'd; take thy own spirit,
> And let no thought infringe thy peace for me;
> I go to have my honours all confirm'd.
>
> (III, i, 12–17)

He does not bother to answer the absurd charges against him, but trusts only in his faith that human law will see their speciousness and thus vindicate him:

> I will not wrong my right and innocence
> With any serious plea in my reply,
> To frustrate breath and fight with terrible shadows,
> That have been forg'd and forc'd against my state,
> But leave all, with my life, to your free censures,
> Only beseeching all your learned judgments,
> Equal and pious conscience, to weigh –
>
> (III, ii, 140–6)

But Chabot is condemned in spite of his faith, and a stage direction tells us that the people show their approval of his sentence.

When the king offers to pardon Chabot he is asserting that the salvation of man depends not upon justice but mercy. This pardon Chabot refuses, for to accept pardon is to deny his innocence:

> I were malicious to myself and desperate
> To force untruths upon my soul, and, when
> 'Tis clear, to confess a shame to exercise
> Your pardon, sir. Were I so foul and monstrous
> As I am given to you, you would commit

> A sin next mine by wronging your own mercy
> To let me draw out impious breath.
>
> (IV, i, 266–72)

This reminds the audience of Chabot's innocence of worldly crime, but also of the pride which causes him to reject the mercy all men need, no matter how virtuous. He appears to be victorious, for the king is forced to examine the circumstances of the trial, and he finds that the judges have been subjected to unlawful pressure. But in Chabot's very victory is also his defeat, for the open corruption of the court to whom he had willingly entrusted his life is now revealed, and the faith in justice by which he had lived is shattered. In the moment of seeming victory he feels the approach of death:

> I never had a fear of the King's justice,
> And yet I know not what creeps o'er my heart
> And leaves an ice beneath it.
>
> (IV, i, 382–4)

Chabot has been saved for the moment, but the faith by which he has lived has been destroyed. The king has merely 'dressed his wounds, I must confess, but made / No cure; they bleed afresh' (V, ii, 75–76).

The collapse of justice is as fully illustrated by the second trial. Poyet is as guilty as Chabot had been innocent, but the attitude of the court remains the same. We have the same pompous garrulity of the Proctor-General and the same abuse heaped upon the victim's head. The two trial scenes—the only prose scenes in the play – were designed obviously to parallel one another, the abuse of the guilty Poyet to recall to the audience that of the innocent Chabot and to remind that there is little real difference in the two situations. The king orders the condemnation of Poyet just as he had ordered that of Chabot; that the trial will be as gross a travesty of justice is implicit in the Advocate's reply to the king's charge:

> He shall be guilty of what you please. I am studied
> In him, sir; I will squeeze his villanies,
> And urge his acts so home into his bowels,

> The force of it shall make him hang himself,
> And save the law a labour.
>
> (IV, i, 401–5)

Chabot is innocent, Poyet guilty, but the law will find only what
the king pleases, for the king is the supreme executor of the law,
and he shares in the general corruption of an imperfect world. It
is this realization which destroys Chabot.

The death scene is entirely Chapman's invention, for there is no
warrant for it in Pasquier, and it certainly is not required by the
historical allegory. It is a dramatic symbol of the collapse of the
ideal of justice for which Chabot had stood. His death is the climax
of Chabot's education, for he has learned that perfect justice is a
mere illusion in an imperfect world. The meeting with Allegre is
introduced to show the cost in physical suffering which Chabot's
test of justice has occasioned:

> Good my lord, let not
> The thought of what I suffer'd dwell upon
> Your memory; they could not punish more
> Than what my duty did oblige to bear
> For you and justice.
>
> (V, iii, 22–26)

There is a pathetic irony in the reward Allegre will receive for
his services; he will serve a new master more difficult than the
master for whom he has suffered. He now asks the crucial question
in the minds of the audience:

> but there's something in
> Your looks presents more fear than all the malice
> Of my tormentors could affect my soul with:
> That paleness, and other forms you wear,
> Would well become a guilty admiral, and one
> Lost to his hopes and honour, not the man
> Upon whose life the fury of injustice,
> Arm'd with fierce lightning, and the power of thunder,
> Can make no breach. I was not rack'd till now:
> There's more death in that falling eye then all
> Rage ever yet brought forth. What accident, sir, can blast,
> Can be so black and fatal, to distract
> The calm, the triumph, that should sit upon
> Your noble brow?
>
> (V, iii, 26–39)

Chabot's reply is not that of a victorious conqueror of injustice.
It is the reply of one who has been struck the mortal blow which is
the loss of the faith by which he has lived:

> Allegre, thou dost bear thy wounds upon thee
> In wide and spacious characters; but in
> The volume of my sadness, thou dost want
> An eye to read; an open force hath torn
> Thy manly sinews, which some time may cure;
> The engine is not seen that wounds thy master
> Past all the remedy of art or time,
> The flatteries of court, of fame or honours.

(V, iii, 44–51)

To describe this inner wound Chabot now uses the very symbol of
the tree which in an earlier time (II, iii, 29–35) he had used to
boast of the innocence which would preserve him in spite of all:

> Thus in the summer a tall flourishing tree,
> Transplanted by strong hand, with all her leaves
> And blooming pride upon her, makes a show
> Of Spring, tempting the eye with wanton blossom;
> But not the sun, with all her amorous smiles,
> The dews of morning, or the tears of night,
> Can root her fibres in the earth again,
> Or make her bosom kind to growth and bearing:
> But the tree withers; and those very beams
> That once were natural warmth to her soft verdure,
> Dry up her sap, and shoot a fever through
> The bark and rind, till she becomes a burthen
> To all which gave her life; so Chabot, Chabot –

(V, iii, 52–64)

That the death of Chabot is the collapse of the ideal of justice is
affirmed by the king himself:

> I see it fall;
> For justice being the prop of every kingdom,
> And mine broke, violating him that was
> The knot and contract of it all in him.

(V, iii, 174–7)

For this destruction of justice the king would blame Poyet, but
the audience knows that Poyet is not to blame, for the inadequacy
of human justice is in the very nature of things. The final plea of
Chabot is that Poyet be granted mercy:

> I observe
> A fierce and killing wrath engender'd in you;
> For my sake, as you wish me strength to serve you,
> Forgive your Chancellor; let not the story
> Of Phillip Chabot, read hereafter, draw
> A tear from any family. I beseech
> Your royal mercy on his life and free
> Remission of all seizure upon his state;
> I have no comfort else.
>
> (V, iii, 189–97)

And he dies not with an expression of pride in his own innocence, but kneeling rather in a final gesture of obedience to the king:

> Sir, I must kneel to thank you,
> It is not seal'd else; your blest hand; live happy.
> May all you trust have no less faith than Chabot!
>
> (V, iii, 199–201)

This final 'faith' is not the pride by which once he had stood, but rather the simple trusting fidelity to his king with which he dies. Chabot had sought to live by a code of perfect justice. He had put his faith in such justice to the trial, and through its bitter outcome he has come to see that justice depends upon human instruments, and that these share in the general imperfection of the world. Man's only hope in a fallen world is the love and mercy of his king and his fellow men. The play is not, as most critics have supposed, Chapman's plea for a perfect human justice. It is rather his tragic statement of its inevitable imperfection.

CHAPTER THREE

Thomas Heywood

I

The most prolific dramatist by far of the entire Elizabethan and Jacobean period was Thomas Heywood, having had a hand, by his own account, in some two hundred and twenty plays. His career, like that of George Chapman, spans the final years of Elizabeth's reign, all of that of James, and extends in fact through most of the Caroline era, for Heywood lived until 1641, surviving into an age when the plays he had written at the beginning of his career were already an anachronism. The greatest of his achievements, *A Woman Killed with Kindness*, was written probably in the same year as Chapman's *Bussy D'Ambois*, but here the parallel between the two men ends, for Heywood remained the apostle of a Renaissance cosmic optimism throughout his long career. He is still, however, entirely a product of his times, for while his writings show a constant reaffirmation of order and degree, of traditional moral values in traditional terms, into his greatest plays there sometimes creeps, perhaps in spite of his avowed didactic purposes, a reflection of the contradictions and ambiguities of his time.

It is probably because his outlook is so different from those of his greater Jacobean contemporaries that Professor Ellis-Fermor omitted Heywood from her classic study of the Jacobean drama. He stands indeed apart from the dramatists we are considering, but if we would have a proper estimate of the moral climate of Jacobean tragedy he cannot be ignored. Although he left no monuments like those of Webster or Middleton, he probably enjoyed a greater popularity than either of them, and he continued to write for the stage after both were dead. Heywood is important because he may illuminate for us a facet of the moral and intellectual milieu of Jacobean tragedy of which we can have no awareness while we restrict our vision to the greater artistic achievements of his contemporaries. Heywood is one who doggedly continued to assert the moral values of an earlier age in a new world in which they no longer had great meaning.

Charles Lamb may have most perfectly summed up the significance of Heywood when he called him a prose Shakespeare. He has been celebrated for the realism of his scenes of Elizabethan life and for the gentle sentimentality of his romantic plots; he may be even more important as one whose imitation of Shakespeare led him to reflect in more prosaic terms a moral viewpoint which we associate with the greatest plays of his master. Like Shakespeare, Heywood was conservative. He saw the universe as the ordered creation of a loving God, every part of which was related to every other, and all joined together in a great cosmic harmony. His tragedies, like Shakespeare's, are concerned with evil as a violation of this order, and they end with the restoration of order by the working out of evil itself in accord with a divine providence. What in Shakespeare emerges, however, as the poet's comprehensive vision of human destiny, conveyed in striking emotional terms, appears in Heywood in the terms of the Elizabethan devotional and homiletic tract.

II

A Woman Killed with Kindness has not generally been admired for its moral content; indeed this has appeared to most critics as bordering close to the absurd. T. S. Eliot has held that the interest of the play is sentimental rather than moral, for 'there is no reality of moral synthesis; to inform the verse there is no vision'.[1] If the play achieves any greatness, it is in the few moments of dramatic realism which enable us to feel the sorrow and regret of Frankford and his wife with an immediate emotional intensity, in the delicacy and refinement of the play's sentiment, and in some passages of poetry where Heywood reaches an aesthetic range he never elsewhere approached. Although it is as deliberately didactic as any play of Chapman's, the morality this play preaches is that of the pulpit, and in its circumscribed domestic setting it fails to relate this morality to any larger cosmic design. There is, as Eliot again

[1] *Selected Essays*, p. 176.

has put it, 'no supernatural music from behind the wings'. We are shown a portrait of sin and repentance, and the way to heaven is indicated to us in conventional terms, but we are afforded no real insight into the relation of man to his universe. That it is tragedy at all has been denied frequently, for if Frankford is the hero, he never loses anything but his domestic content; even as domestic tragedy we need only compare it to *Othello* to see how barren it is of real cosmic scope.[1]

That the play in its specific thematic statement reflects the commonplaces of Elizabethan popular theology has been demonstarted in some detail.[2] The basic situation of the main plot involves the traditional conflict between good and evil; Mistress Frankford and Wendoll succumb to the attractions of lust, are punished and made to see the folly of their fall from virtue and the threat of damnation which it has involved. There has been much useless debate about the credibility of the seduction of Mistress Frankford. T. S. Eliot has held it perfectly reasonable in terms of ordinary life situation, while others have sought to explain it in terms of the 'Renaissance attitude' towards women which relegated them to a lower intellectual plane than men as creatures more subject to animal passion.[3] But Heywood is concerned here with portraying the kind of fall from virtue of which it was axiomatic in Christian doctrine that all men were capable. In terms of the tradition of moral *exemplum* which conditions the play, no further explanation is necessary.

As Heywood's answer to the fact of evil in the world, we have Master Frankford, a model of the Christian gentleman held up for the audience as an example of how one must act if evil is to be thwarted. As a gentleman he thinks of his honour which must be protected, but his primary concern is for the salvation of his wife's soul. When he kills her with kindness, he is acting entirely out of love for her; in opposition to the code which demanded blood revenge, he asserts the contrary Christian doctrine of forgiveness

---

[1] See Moody E. Prior, *The Language of Tragedy*, pp. 95–96.
[2] H. H. Adams, *English Domestic Or, Homiletic Tragedy 1575 to 1642* (New York, 1943), pp. 144–59.
[3] See Hallett D. Smith, 'A Woman Killed with Kindness,' *PMLA*, LIII (1938), 138–47. Smith relates Mistress Frankford to such sinful women as Elstred, Rosamund Clifford and Jane Shore.

and reconciliation. Frankford acts to bring his wife to a state of sincere repentance, and only upon her death bed, when he is assured of her soul's salvation, does he at last forgive her. If he appears as priggish, rigid, and mechanical, it is again because Heywood is concerned primarily with making his simple theological point. What greatness the play achieves is in spite of the author's theological purpose and not because of it. This again is an index of its inadequacy as tragedy.

The sub-plot has been dismissed usually as irrelevant matter which Heywood used merely to fill in his five act structure, and whose general inadequacy almost succeeds in destroying the play. But Eliot, I believe, is wrong on both counts when he writes (p. 177) that 'Middleton's *The Changeling* . . . must share with *A Woman Killed with Kindness* the discredit of having the weakest underplot of any important play in the whole Elizabethan repertory'. Melodramatic, gauche and often ridiculous as Heywood's story of the unfortunate Sir Charles Mountford and his sister may be, it is nevertheless joined thematically to the main plot,[1] for its subject also is the preservation of honour and the destruction of evil through kindness and love. Middleton's two plots in *The Changeling* are also closely joined, as we shall see, and although Heywood was a lesser dramatist, he was at least experienced enough in the theatre to recognize that such thematic linking was a principal element in the greater multi-plot plays of his time. He had the example of his master Shakespeare always before him.

We must recognize at once that Heywood's sub-plot represents the kind of sentimental romance for which this author had a particular affection, and which was particularly cherished by the lower middle class audiences who frequented the Red Bull theatre. It is of the same generic stock as the Jane Shore story which Heywood permitted to distort his earlier *Edward IV* plays out of all proportion. The familiar story of the ever-loving virtuous sister brought to the point where to save her brother she must sacrifice her chastity to the villain is a perfect example of folk romance, and it is in keeping not only with such romance but with

[1] See Freda L. Townsend, 'The Artistry of Heywood's Double Plots,' *PQ*, XXV (1946), 97–119.

Heywood's particular moral attitudes that she should be saved at last by the miraculous power of her virtue to work a transformation in her oppressor and assure the final happiness of all. The moral premises upon which the story is based are rigid and old-fashioned, but they represent ideas as dear to a lower class audience as are the theological principles of Master Frankford. As a man of honour Sir Charles cannot accept a kindness from his enemy. He must repay Sir Francis with the chastity of his sister, the only good he possesses, and when he has delivered his sister in payment of his debt he must slay himself, just as his sister must kill herself before the actual loss of her chastity: 'Her honour she will hazard, though not lose: To bring me out of debt, her rigorous hand / Will pierce her heart' (V, i).

Heywood is not concerned with the contradictions and ambiguities in the situation – that in surrendering his sister Charles may actually be forfeiting the honour he seeks to preserve, or that by killing herself Susan will actually forfeit the family honour by cheating her brother's creditor. Such fine considerations are alien to the spirit of folk romance, and the audience caught up in the sentiment of the action does not stop to consider them. Like the courtesy of Arveragus in Chaucer's *Franklin's Tale*, that of Sir Charles is intended as an example of the highest type of honour and magnanimity. It belongs to the same romantic tradition as the offer of Arveragus, and it has the same effect: to shock the demanding adversary so profoundly that he must respond with a similar act of magnanimity:

> Stern heart, relent;
> Thy former cruelty at length repent.
> Was ever known, in any former age,
> Such honourable wrested courtesy?
> Lands, honours, life, and all the world forego,
> Rather than stand engaged to such a foe.
>
> (V, i)

Thus in the sub-plot as well as in the main-plot the practice of a consistent Christian virtue has the power to destroy evil in the world. In the main plot this is shown primarily in terms of a conventional Christianity which upholds the salvation of the soul as the greatest good, and counsels love and forgiveness as the instruments with which man must oppose evil; in the sub-plot it is shown in terms of a conventional notion of honour and gentility which in the rapidly changing England of Heywood's day belonged already to the past.

Evil in Heywood appears as a temporary disruption of the natural goodness of the world. Even Wendoll, who comes as close to a villain as any character in Heywood's works, is pursued by remorse. Heywood is incapable of creating an Iago to symbolize an unalterable demonic force forever confronting mankind, although in the temptation of Mistress Frankford by Wendoll he is able to suggest the eternal temptation by Satan to which mankind is subject. Mrs Frankford is a model of virtue until she commits her single sin, and then the rest of her life must be devoted to sincere Christian repentance. In *The English Traveller* Mistress Wincott also is guilty only of a momentary departure from virtue for which she must atone with her life as soon as her sin has been revealed. Delavil, the false friend and seducer, must flee in remorse like Wendoll, and the injured Young Geraldine, like Frankford, never once thinks of taking any action against the woman and the friend who have betrayed him. He is confident always that heaven will be his avenger. In the sub-plot of that play also, the ease with which Old Lionel pardons the son who has tricked and defrauded him again illustrates the typical Heywood motif of love and Christian charity destroying evil and restoring harmony on earth.

Yet the very need which Heywood felt to reassert these traditional beliefs may be an indication of the particular confusion and uncertainty of the age in which he lived, and the persistency of his affirmation may suggest the wide-spread dissent against which it was directed. We may, in fact, find in Heywood, particularly in *A Woman Killed with Kindness* and *The English Traveller*, alongside the optimistic Christian moralizing, signs of the uncertainty against which Heywood asserts his optimistic vision. Woven into the structure of his greatest plays there is that theme of the confusion of appearance with reality which is a constant theme in the Jacobean Shakespeare, the inability of man so often to distinguish virtue from its opposite, and out of this inability his tragedy pro-

ceeding.[1] This in itself is a traditional Christian motif, springing
from the notion that man chooses evil through the inadequacy of
his reason which permits him to mistake it for the good. The fall
of Eve in the garden of Eden traditionally had been explained in
these terms. Yet its emphasis in Heywood and in his Jacobean
contemporaries is an index of the particular pessimism of their age.

The ease with which a virtuous wife may become an unfaithful
one, while it may cause Frankford to question the reliability of his
own perception and judgment, is not to be taken as evidence that
the initial virtue of Mistress Frankford is any the less real. When
she is described in the very first speech of the play as

> the chief
> Of all the sweet felicities on earth,
> . . . a fair, a chaste, and loving wife;
> Perfection all, all truth, all ornament.

(I, i)

Heywood intends no irony. This is important dramatic exposition,
to emphasize the perfection of the heroine which we have no
reason to doubt before her fall. The tragedy is not that the husband is deceived by any falsehood in her initial virtuous appearance, but rather that such virtue may so easily undergo corruption.
When Frankford beholds the fall of his wife he is brought to an
awareness of evil's reality in the world and of the weakness of
human judgment as a defence against it. When first he is given
reason to suspect his wife, he questions the fallibility of his
judgment:

> Though I durst pawn my life, and on their faith
> Hazard the dear salvation of my soul,
> Yet in my trust I may be too secure.
> May this be true? O, may it, can it be?
> Is it by any wonder possible?
> Man, woman, what thing mortal can we trust,

[1] This theme has been emphasized in particular by Patricia Meyer Spacks, 'Honor
and Perception in "A Woman Killed with Kindness",' *MLQ*, XX (1959), 321–32,
but I believe that Mrs Spacks distorts the play in extending this theme to conclude
that 'the play presents a unified, if sombre, vision of a world governed by considerations other than honour', finding in Heywood a kind of cynicism which runs
contrary to the dominant impression not only of this play but of every other of his
extant works.

> When friends and bosom wives prove so unjust?
>
> (III, ii)

The answer to his question will be in the confirmation of his
suspicions. The awareness to which it will bring him is necessary,
however, to his performance of his Christian duties; he must
recognize his own human fallibility and the ever present power of
evil.

Where Frankford is truly deceived is in his judgment of
Wendoll, for here what he perceives at first to be virtue is only
the outward mask of virtue which hides an inner evil. This is
made clear by the suspicions of the servant, Nicholas, who sees
from the first what Wendoll truly is, and who finally brings about
his unmasking. Wendoll seems to stand, as I have suggested, for
the tempter Satan who brought Eve to disaster in the Garden of
Eden, for he tempts Mrs Frankford in the same manner. If we
are to find in the play a larger allegorical overtone relating the
fall and salvation of one wife to the fall and salvation of all mankind, certainly Frankford has many elements of the Christ-figure.
The Satanic aspect of Wendoll appears in the speech with which
he leaves the play:

> She's gone to death; I live to want and woe;
> Her life, her sins, and all upon my head.
> And I must now go wander, like a Cain,
> In foreign countries and remoted climes,
> Where the report of my ingratitude
> Cannot be heard. I'll over first to France,
> And so to Germany and Italy;
> Where when I have recovered, and by travel
> Gotten those perfect tongues, and that these rumours
> May in their height abate, I will return:
> And I divine (however now dejected)
> My worth and parts being by some great man praised,
> At my return I may in court be raised.
>
> (V, iii)

Heywood, of course, is reflecting upon the court corruption of
his own day, but while Wendoll must suffer for his sin, and he
is 'Pursued with horror of a guilty soul / And with the sharp
scourge of repentance lashed', Heywood is suggesting also that
Wendoll will rise again because he stands for a kind of evil

which finally cannot be destroyed. This is but the merest hint, and I would not emphasize it very strongly, but Wendoll does rise again, in fact, in the Delavil of *The English Traveller*, modelled closely upon the earlier figure. When we read the two plays in close succession we feel the existence of a tempter of mankind constantly reappearing with a different name but otherwise unchanged. In *The English Traveller* the themes of virtue's corruption and the failure of human perception are repeated in very similar terms in the seduction of Mistress Wincott by Delavil, and the inability of man to rely upon his own judgment and senses is particularly illustrated by the deception practised upon Old Lionel.

In the inability of Sir Charles in the sub-plot of *A Woman Killed with Kindness* to recognize the malice of his liberator from prison, and particularly in his inability to perceive the treachery of Shafton who lends him money, we have again the theme of the deception in outward appearances, and in this instance it is combined with protest against some of the most socially destructive practices of Heywood's age, the corruption in the courts, and the widespread depredation wrought by usury. The rejection of Susan's pleas for help by those whom the Mountfords had most befriended in the past is a familiar folk-tale motif but, it emphasizes also the corroding forces of greed and ingratitude in society, just as Sir Charles' determination to hold on to his meagre remnant of land calls attention to the gradual passing of the great country estates into the hands of the London merchant classes, which conservatives like Heywood witnessed with a particular horror. It is not to be taken as a suggestion that Sir Charles values his land more than he does his sister's life and chastity. Heywood never ceases to proclaim his traditional Christian morality, to preach the power of love and honour to work a reformation in the world, but he is more keenly aware of the evils of his age – perhaps of the contradictions inherent in its very code of morality and honour – than most critics have been willing to allow. In this he shows that in his own peculiar way he is very much a part of his Jacobean milieu.

III

A Woman Killed with Kindness and *The English Traveller* are probably Heywood's two best plays, but it is not because either of them fully attains the dimension of tragedy. They are both genuinely Christian in their point of view, and they are immediately and obviously concerned with stating an explicit moral position. They remain, in spite of this, domestic plays in which the dramatist makes little attempt to relate his morality to any larger cosmic scheme. Only the immediate family is concerned, never, as in Shakespeare, the state and the physical universe as well. In only one play did Heywood attempt to write tragedy of real cosmic range, and although this play has remained among the least respected works in his canon, it seems to be the play which he himself regarded most seriously as his contribution to the highest realm of English drama. Heywood refers to his *Rape of Lucrece* as 'A True Roman Tragedy', placing it thus in the company of what Renaissance neo-classicism saw as the highest type of drama; it is the type to which Ben Jonson himself, literary arbiter of the age, aspired. Heywood's Roman tragedy is a far lesser work than either of Jonson's, but it does attempt a cosmic range of which Jonson was incapable.

The many printings of *The Rape of Lucrece* suggest that it was far more popular in its own day than it has been in ours.[1] By recent critics it has been dismissed usually as a parody of the classics or as a crude attempt to cater to the lower tastes of Heywood's plebeian audience. A. M. Clark, a very lukewarm defender, condemns it as tragedy, but argues that it must be read as a 'chronicle history'.[2] The many songs of the comical Valerius – which must have catered to a popular demand in Heywood's day – have been censured in particular as inappropriate to the seriousness of the play's subject. Of their poor taste there can be no doubt, but we must do Heywood the justice of observing that the songs are later additions to the play, and that when they were inserted they were concentrated in those central scenes where the dramatist wishes to stress the escape of the Roman lords into wanton amusement

[1] Allan Holaday, ed. *The Rape of Lucrece* (Urbana, Ill., 1950), has suggested that this play was revised by Heywood in 1607 from a play he had written at the very beginning of his career, around 1594. If this be so–and Holaday's evidence is very tenuous indeed – the strong influence of Shakespeare's *Macbeth* (1606) in the play would suggest that the 1607 revision was a very thorough one.

[2] *Thomas Heywood, Playwright and Miscellanist* (Oxford, 1931), pp. 220–1.

and self-indulgence in the face of Tarquin's tyranny. The change
of Valerius himself from statesman into singing fool is one of the
reflections in the life of individual man of the corruption in the
universal order which springs from Tarquin's tyranny. The
transformation of the Roman lords, as I shall try to show, is an
essential element in the total moral vision of the play. The most
offensive song of all, the three part catch in which Pompey the
clown informs Valerius and Horatius of the rape (2296–343) is
a means of exposition which, in spite of its crudity and abominable
taste, is not entirely alien to the dramatic tradition in which Heywood worked.[1] That the play is marred by many and obvious
artistic defects does not alter the fact that in its totality it represents Heywood's effort to embody in drama a more comprehensive view of man's relation to his universe than he ever elsewhere attempted.

Certainly Heywood is no Shakespeare. But we must note that
in spite of the many irrelevancies in the work, its often sentimental
and ineffectual verse, the play nevertheless has a central unifying
theme. It is not, as Holaday calls it, merely a loosely connected
series of scenes which follow Livy's account of the reign and fall
of the Tarquins, the political events having little connection with
the central episode which gives the tragedy its title. We must do
Heywood the justice of observing that the political and private
affairs of his play are not haphazardly thrown together. They are
closely related to one another by a distinct moral vision to which
each contributes. This is established in the opening scene of the
play when Tullia says, 'A kingdom's quest, makes sons and
fathers foes' (112), linking the unlawful act of political usurpation
to the severance of the natural bond between father and son, just
as Shakespeare links his political and personal themes in *King
Lear*. Corruption in the state must be reflected in corruption in
the family, in the destruction of the normal impulses of man, and
finally in the rape of Lucrece.

The text of 1608, whether or not it be a revision of an earlier
play, shows the strong influence of Shakespeare's *Macbeth*. This
involves more than a matter of phraseology, or of Heywood's
basing his Tarquin-Tullia relation upon that of Macbeth and his

[1] See M. C. Bradbrook, *Themes and Conventions of Elizabethan Tragedy*, p. 110.

wife, as most commentators have observed. Heywood attempted
also to embody in his tragedy the moral viewpoint of Shakespeare's masterpiece. *The Rape of Lucrece*, like *Macbeth*, is concerned with the destruction of order and its restitution through
the working out of evil, on the personal, the political and the
cosmic levels. When Tullia treads upon the skull of her father
and drives her chariot over his body, Heywood is not merely
catering to the sordid tastes of a depraved audience. He is creating
in terms of his own theatrical tradition a symbol of human sacrilege
which will culminate in war and tyranny for Rome, will destroy
the manhood of the Roman lords, and will violate the sanctity of
the family in the rape of Lucrece. The visit to the Delphic oracle
is not brought in primarily to satisfy the Jacobean fondness for
stage magic. The oracle sounds the motif of divine retribution and
the purging of sin: 'Then Rome her ancient honours wins, / When
she is purg'd from Tullia's sins' (711–12). The oracle heralds a
universal restitution of order which has been destroyed by
hatred's triumph over love, and it prepares for the significant
couplet which ends the play:

> March on to Rome, Jove be our guard and guide,
> That hath in us, veng'd rape, and punished pride.
> (2888–9)

The play ends on the note of divine providence bringing about
the restitution of order, deriving good out of evil itself, meting
out rewards and punishments in accord with the justice of a
perfect heavenly plan.

In the opening scene of the play Heywood makes clear the
leading motifs of his work, and he uses the commentary of the
feigned madman, Brutus Junior, to drive them home. When
Tarquin and Tullia unlawfully seek the throne, they are striving
like Shakespeare's Lord and Lady Macbeth, to rise above the
station which in the divine plan it is their lot to occupy, and such
striving can only shatter the harmony of all creation. As they plot
the usurpation, they make clear to the audience that this act must
also involve a severance of the natural human feelings. The aged
king Servius is Tullia's father, but 'who aspires, / Mounts by the

lives of fathers, sons and sires' (116–17). They must 'despise a father for a crown' (119). Unlike the murder of Duncan, that of Servius is not undertaken merely as a means to kingship, to be executed reluctantly and in spite of strong opposing feelings. Heywood is cruder than Shakespeare in emphasizing his point: Tullia exults in the desecration of her father as fully as she exults in being queen, for the two acts are inseparably linked. She urges her husband to

> let his mangled body lie,
> And with his base confederates strew the streets,
> That in disgrace of his usurped pride,
> We o'er his trunk may in our chariot ride:
> For mounted like a queen 'twould do me good
> To wash my coach-naves in my father's blood.

> (346–51)

Tullia is a mechanical and lifeless figure beside Lady Macbeth, but Heywood is deeply concerned with her dramatic symbolism. Usurpation and patricide, the public and the private sin, in her are closely linked, the one dependent upon the other.

The rest of the play may be summed up as an exploration of the implications of this initial act, with its public and its private consequences portrayed always in close relation to one another. There will be treachery and tyranny on the level of the state, issuing in treachery and human desecration on the level of personal human relations. We are reminded by Brutus that in this initial sin is also implicit the destruction of the Tarquins, for evil set in motion must work out its course, and when it has done so order will be restored, for a just and benevolent God will punish sinners and preserve the harmony of creation:

> Jove art thou just; hast thou reward for piety?
> And for offence no vengeance? or canst punish
> Felons and pardon traitors? chastise murderers,
> And wink at parricides? if thou be worthy,
> As well we know thou art, to fill the throne
> Of all eternity, then with that hand
> That flings the trisulk thunder, let the pride
> Of these our irreligious monarchizers
> Be crown'd in blood.

> (378–86)

The sin of Tarquin and Tullia is compared to that of 'those giants that wag'd war against the Gods' (363), an equally unnatural act, and Heywood dwells upon all of the gruesome details so as to stress the horror of the crime, and the particular violation of nature which can permit a woman to be its author:

> but the queen,
> A woman, fie fie: did not this she-parricide
> Add to her father's wounds? and when his body
> Lay all besmeared and stained in the blood royal,
> Did not this monster, this infernal hag,
> Make her unwilling charioteer drive on,
> And with his shod wheels crush her father's bones?
> Break his craz'd skull, and dash his sparkled brains
> Upon the pavements, whilst she held the reins?
> The affrighted sun at this abhorred object,
> Put on a mask of blood, and yet she blushed not.
>
> (367-77)

The redness of the terrified sun shows nature itself recoiling, and this is Heywood's way of relating the corruption of the physical universe itself to that of the individual, the family and the state. Shakespeare, in the same manner, had dwelled upon the unnatural phenomena which accompanied the murder of Duncan, the clouds hanging over Scotland, blotting out the sun, and the horses devouring one another. The justice of God upon which Brutus calls will be vindicated in the destruction of the Tarquins, but until heaven is ready to act the entire universe will suffer corruption. The madness of Brutus is a symbol of this general corruption which persists while the Tarquins rule, for when the final sacrilege has been enacted and heaven is ready for vengeance, Brutus throws off his madness and, like Shakespeare's Macduff, becomes the instrument which heaven uses to destroy the tyrants and restore the universe to order.

The civil uprising against the Tarquins springs directly from the personal crime against Lucrece, while her rape is merely the reflection upon the personal level of the initial political crime: 'Oh who but Sextus could commit such waste? / On one so fair, so kind, so truly chaste?' (1954-55). Only the creature of Tarquin's tyranny and usurpation can commit the personal outrage, and this crime, in turn, becomes the spur which leads finally to the restoration of political order. By this pattern of cause and effect Heywood relates the diverse elements of his play as surely as Shakespeare relates the murder of Duncan to the wanton slaughter of Macduff's children.

After the opening scene, with its symbolic statement of the unifying theme, the play falls naturally into two movements. First we are shown the issue of the initial act in a corruption both of Rome and of the private virtue of her citizens. The statesman Valerius becomes a fool, 'from a toward hopeful gentleman, / Transhaped to a mere ballater' (540–1), as the misguided strength of Tarquin becomes the weakness of all Rome:

> Tarquin's ability will in the weal,
> Beget a weak unable impotence:
> His strength, make Rome and our dominions weak,
> His soaring high make us to flag our wings,
> And fly close by the earth: his golden feathers
> Are of such vastness, that they spread like sails,
> And so becalm us that we have not air
> Able to raise our plumes, to taste the pleasures
> of our own elements.
>
> (473–80)

The careful antitheses in this speech reflect the perversion of order which continues to be emphasized until its most horrible expression in the rape of Lucrece. Then begins a second movement which details the restitution of order through God's providence. Brutus throws off the madness which has been the symbol of his impotence, and the heroic feats of Horatius and Mutius Scevola, which in Livy occur much later and have no relation to the rape of Lucrece, are drawn into the play to emphasize the reassertion of human dignity and the heroic stature of ancient Romans which must accompany the restoration of order to the state. Through both of these movements there is a constant emphasis upon the close relation between the public and the private spheres of action.

The visit of Brutus, Sextus and Aruns to the Delphic oracle serves an important function. The oracle not only stresses the fall of Tarquin as the price of Rome's redemption, but he places the succession to the throne in terms of personal human affection:

'He that first shall kiss his mother, / Shall be powerful.' Only
Brutus perceives the meaning of the oracle and he kisses his mother
earth, assuring to the audience the eventual restitution of order to
Rome. He emphasizes also the symbolic implications of the
oracle, for love of mother is seen as closely related both to love
of country and love of the physical earth, all three aspects of love
being tied together in a harmonious cosmic unity. For Aruns and
Sextus, children of disorder, the oracle leads only to the desecration of maternal love, for brother struggles against brother for
the mother's kiss which each values only as the means to kingship.
Sextus vows revenge upon his brother who bests him in this, and
he, in fact, refuses his mother's kiss when it is offered only as a
symbol of maternal love and not as assurance of the crown. This
desecration of human value repeats the motif of the opening
scene. The hatred of Aruns and Sextus is 'unnatural enmity'
(890); it is 'Hate, born from love' (891). In its general statement
about human love and its relation to the love of his people which
is the cardinal requirement of the virtuous king, this scene shows
a surer capacity for symbolic statement than critics usually have
been willing to allow to Heywood.

The sins of Tarquin and Tullia spread through the common-
wealth, infusing Rome with corruption. The defection of Sextus
to the Gabines is the first fruit of his quarrel with his brother.
It represents rebellion against the homeland as well as the unnatural
turning of the son against the father, as the father must turn
against the son:

> Does the proud boy confederate with our foes?
> Attend us lords, we must new battle wage,
> And with bright arms confront the proud boy's rage.
>
> (944–6)

When Sextus betrays his newfound allies and is welcomed back
by Tarquin with new honours as the reward for his treachery, we
see the moral corruption which has replaced the ancient ideal of
Roman honour.

To emphasize this all-pervasive corruption, Heywood in the
central scenes of his play stresses the idleness and dalliance of the
great men of Rome. They neglect their ancient offices and spend
their time in idle amusement away from court. Scevola, who later

is to reassert his nobility, under Tarquin's rule laments that 'The time that should have been seriously spent in the state-house, I have learned securely to spend in a wenching house, and now I profess myself anything but a statesman' (1003–5). This willing neglect of civil duty, which springs from Tarquin's initial crime, is what makes possible the rape of Lucrece, completing the chain of cause and effect. There is a mood of dalliance and amusement-seeking among the Roman generals in the camp before Ardea when the fateful wager is made, through which Sextus gains his first admittance to the house of Lucrece. The very treachery of Sextus against the Gabines has led to the siege of Ardea in the first place, for his treachery has been rewarded with a generalship, and his reconciliation with his father has led to the campaign against the neighbour nations. Tarquin boasts to Porsenna of the exploits of the Roman army which his son commands, but the generals of this army have abandoned the soldier's virtues, and the issue of their campaign will be only the rape of Lucrece.

That the Roman generals have been infused with the corruption out of which their very campaign has issued is made clear by the dialogue between two common soldiers with which Heywood prefaces the crucial banquet scene. While the generals revel, only the common soldier stands guard against the enemy:

> there's no commander
> Of any note, but revels with the prince.
>
> (1377–8)

> thus must poor soldiers do,
> Whil'st their commanders are with dainties fed,
> And sleep on down, the earth must be our bed.
>
> (1386–8)

This episode is inserted not merely to offer a plea for the common soldier, as is usually supposed, but to throw into sharper focus the negligent unmanlike activity of the generals which will make possible the rape of Lucrece.

The personal effects of Tarquin's tyranny and the military campaign which results from it are made clear by Lucrece herself. They separate the husband from the wife and make possible the desecration of the home:

With no unkindness we should our lords upbraid,
Husbands and kings must always be obeyed.
Nothing save the high business of the state,
And the charge given him at Ardea's siege,
Could have made Collatine so much digress,
From the affection that he bears his wife.
But subjects must excuse when kings claim power.

(1691-7)

She indicates here the close relation of her coming disaster to the power exerted by an illicit kingship. If this soliloquy has any function, it is to make clear how public power impinges upon private life, how an evil king and his evil son pervert the husband's role as his wife's protector and leave open the way to sacrilegious outrage. There may be some symbolic implication in the fact that it is Collatine's ring which enables Sextus to gain entrance to Lucrece. 'Without that key you had not entered here' (1792), she says, indicating that the tyrant has usurped the husband's natural role: 'without this from his hand, Sextus this night could not have entered here: no not the king himself' (1162-4). Collatine himself, by the dissipation and dereliction of duty he has shared with the other lords, has prepared the way for his wife's disaster, but his abandonment of duty has been the result of Tarquin's initial crime.

Lucrece from the very beginning of the play has stood as a symbol of the virtue to which the rule of the Tarquins stands opposed. If she seems priggish in her lecturing of her servants on chastity, it is simply that Heywood is trying to stress the ordered regularity of the household she rules, as opposed to the patent disorder in the Rome of the Tarquins. She is as consistent in her moral position as Master Frankford is in his, and Heywood is more interested in making clear this moral position than he is in creating a realistic character. It is the destruction of the chastity of Lucrece and the virtue for which it stands which finally causes Brutus to abandon his pose of madness and with the other Roman lords to throw off the slothful neglect of duty which had been the symbol of the infusion of Tarquin's sin into the body politic. He at last is able to arouse his compatriots to action:

As you are Romans, and esteem your fame

More than your lives, all humorous toys set off.
Of madding, singing, smiling and what else,
Receive your native valours, be your selves,
And join with Brutus in the just revenge
Of this chaste ravished lady, swear.

(2473–8)

The rape of Lucrece is the spark which revives the ancient valour
of the Romans; it is the culmination of evil which gives birth at
last to good. In asserting their valour the Roman lords execute
the vengeance not of private citizens, but of divine providence.
'Leave all to Heaven' (1221) had been Collatine's answer to the
tyranny of Tarquin, in accord with the traditional Tudor doctrine
of passive obedience which Heywood always espouses.[1] When the
Roman lords now march against Tarquin, it is as heaven's instruments destroying the usurper, not as private citizens opposing
their king. Brutus and Collatine assert divine purpose as surely as
do Shakespeare's Macduff and Malcolm when they march against
the usurper Macbeth. Brutus is heaven's answer to sacrilege and
disorder: 'We'll murder murder, and base rape shall bleed' (2544).

The horror of rebellion is a common theme in Heywood, as we
might expect from his intense loyalty to the ideals of Tudor
absolutism. To make his position clear in *The Rape of Lucrece*, he
deliberately raises the issue of the exact nature of the insurrection
against the Tarquins when he has Sextus accuse the Roman lords
of treason in conventional Tudor terms, linking rebellion against
the king to rebellion against God:

Traitors to heaven: to Tarquin, Rome and us,
Treason to kings doth stretch even to the Gods,
And those high Gods shall take Rome in charge,
Shall punish your rebellion.

(2557–60)

This is the charge which Brutus and Collatine must answer if
their campaign against the Tarquins is to be vindicated. To justify
their position Heywood must make clear that Tarquin is not the

[1] There is clear statement of Heywood's scrupulously orthodox political position
that prayer is man's only recourse against tyranny and that rebellion is the worst of
all possible evils in his historical plays, *Edward IV* and *If You Know Not Me, You
Know Nobody*. See *The English History Play in the Age of Shakespeare* (Princeton, 1957),
pp. 273–8, 218–23.

lawful king which Sextus claims him to be, but rather a usurper who has ruled only through God's sufferance and not as the agent on earth of a benevolent divine will. The rape of Lucrece is now the symbol which exposes the falsehood of Sextus's protestation; it is the sacrilege which defeats the claim of the tyrant to divine protection:

> Oh devil Sextus, speak not thou of Gods,
> Nor cast those false and feigned eyes to heaven,
> Whose rape the furies must torment in hell,
> Of Lucrece, Lucrece.
>
> (2561–4)

Brutus now invokes the prophecy of the oracle. In destroying the Tarquins he is fulfilling the decree of fate, acting as the agent of divine providence, rather than opposing the will of God, of which a rebel against a lawful king in Tudor terms would be guilty:

> Now Sextus where's the oracle, when I kissed
> My mother earth it plainly did foretell,
> My noble virtues did thy sin exceed,
> Brutus should sway, and lust burned Tarquin bleed.
>
> (2585–8)

That the destruction of the Tarquins represents God's vengeance for the initial murder of Servius with which the play began is now made clear by the choral speeches of Valerius and Horatius:

> Now shall the blood of Servius fall as heavy
> As a huge mountain on your tyrant heads, o'erwhelming
> all your glory.
>
> (2589–90)

> .   .   .   .   .   .
> Tullia's guilt, shall be by us revenged that in her pride
> In blood paternal, her rough coach-wheels dyed.
>
> (2591–2)

The image of the mountain crushing the sinner recalls the beginning of the play where the murder of Servius had been compared to the sin of

> Those giants that waged war against the Gods,
> For which the o'erwhelmed mountains hurled by Jove
> To scatter them, and give them timeless graves

Was not more cruel than this butchery.

(363–6)

The Gods now have executed a like revenge. The play's conclusion represents the final working out of the evil with which it began.

To show also that the Romans fight in the service of divine justice and order, Heywood now works into his play the episode so often censured as an extraneous intrusion, the heroic defence of Rome by Horatius at the bridge. The feat is semi-miraculous, and Horatius is acting in answer to the prayer of Brutus:

> Thou Jovial hand hold up thy sceptre high,
> And let not justice be oppressed with pride,
> Oh you penates leave not Rome and us,
> Grasped in the purple hand of death and ruin.

(2616–9)

The self-mutilation of Mutius Scevola is used also to affirm the new heroic valour which now infuses the Roman lords in their desire to avenge the rape of Lucrece. Scevola's heroic act so impresses Porsenna that he spares his life, and moved by the spirit he sees in his opponents, he is prepared for the final reconciliation which will assure peace and stability to the new Rome freed from the tyranny of the Tarquins.

There are extraneous elements in *The Rape of Lucrece*. The mutual destruction of Sextus and Brutus, for instance, while it serves the needs of stage spectacle and adds a moment of dramatic tension at the end, does not further the theme, for it would have been more suitable in this respect had the play ended with Brutus still alive. In spite of such lapses, we can see that the principal events of the play are related to one another by a basic design. The rape of Lucrece is not merely one of a series of sensational episodes; it is the central element of the play which serves to unite the public and the private spheres of action, to tie a private crime to the larger questions of the destiny of Rome and the providence of God. Heywood, like Shakespeare, sees the affairs of men and the affairs of the state as inter-related in a harmonious total order, and the central theme of *The Rape of Lucrece* is the violation of order by the perverted will of man and the restitution of order by a divine providence working through human action.

If *The Rape of Lucrece* is a pedestrian imitation of *Macbeth*, it does nevertheless attempt to give dramatic form to a vision of man's relation to the forces of evil in the world which is distinctly Shakespearian and which, in this respect, sets Heywood apart from his major Jacobean contemporaries.

CHAPTER FOUR

Cyril Tourneur

I

To form an estimate of Cyril Tourneur's contribution to English tragedy has been very difficult, for we know almost nothing about his literary career, and of the two plays usually attributed to him his authorship of one has often been denied. His name appeared on the title page of *The Atheist's Tragedy* when it was printed in 1611, but *The Revenger's Tragedy* was printed anonymously in 1607, and it was not until 1656 that the play was attributed to Tourneur in Edward Archer's play list.[1] Between the two plays there is also a wide diversity in artistic achievement. That *The Atheist's Tragedy* is an inferior work, however, is not necessary evidence of separate authorship. What is perhaps even more striking about these two plays is that each in its own way is a highly moralistic and didactic work, and that they share a crusading missionary tone and a common point of view which renders them more like one another than either is like any of the plays of Tourneur's contemporaries.[2] Taken together the Tourneur plays represent a particular attitude towards the moral issues of their age which renders them virtually unique. Tourneur's answer to social corruption and human debasement is in a return to a primitive Christianity.

[1] On the authorship question see Samuel Schoenbaum, *Middleton's Tragedies, A Critical Study* (New York, 1955), pp. 156–82. Schoenbaum would attribute the play to Middleton, as would R. H. Barker, *Thomas Middleton* (New York, 1958) pp. 64–75, both following E. H. C. Oliphant, *Shakespeare and his Fellow Dramatists* (New York, 1929), II, 93.

[2] Tourneur's authorship of both plays has been argued effectively by Harold Jenkins, 'Cyril Tourneur,' *RES*, XVII (1941), 21–36; U. M. Ellis-Fermor, 'The Imagery of "The Revenger's Tragedie" and "The Atheist's Tragedie",' *MLR*, XLVIII (1953), 129–38; Inga-Stina Ekeblad, 'On the Authorship of "The Revenger's Tragedy",' *English Studies*, XLI (1960), 225–40. In 'An Approach to Tourneur's Imagery', *MLR*, LIV (1959), 489–98, Miss Ekeblad has argued that in both plays imagery is used in the same manner to support a moral theme.

This is not the optimistic Christian religion of Shakespeare or Heywood, with its emphasis upon order and degree and upon the dignity of man and his commanding position in an ordered purposive universe. Tourneur's is the pessimistic Christianity inherent in a large segment of medieval thought, implicit in Augustine and Aquinas, which had its most characteristic expression in the *De Contemptu Mundi* of Pope Innocent III. It shares the same premisses, themselves medieval in origin, of a decaying universe and a degenerate humanity which we have noted in the plays of Chapman, but with none of the characteristic seventeenth-century scepticism. Tourneur's emphasis is upon the baseness and corruption of man as the inheritor of original sin. He stresses man's smallness in the universe, his slavery to the ravages of time, and hence his need to look to the other world as his only hope of felicity. Of this other world there is no doubt. Tourneur's plays employ the traditional devices of hortatory and homiletic literature to argue a Christian point of view which was receiving renewed emphasis as Christian humanism began to decline in the early years of the seventeenth century, but which had always been a part of orthodox Christian belief. In their moral fervour Tourneur's plays have been related to a tradition of complaint and satire extending back to the Middle Ages.[1]

If the earlier of the plays is the greater artistic achievement, it may be in part because of a fresher poetic inspiration which enabled the author to forge his total play as a symbol of his moral point of view, whereas in the later play he fell back upon a method of explicit moralizing, allowing such characters as Charlemont and Castiza to preach his moral doctrine directly to the audience. In *The Revenger's Tragedy* Tourneur uses the devices of poetry to make his audience feel the insignificance of the present world in the light of eternity. He carries his moral theme in his poetic imagery and in the cadence of his lines. *The Atheist's Tragedy* is somewhat weaker in poetic imagery; the author seems to rely rather upon narrative and argument. He uses the devices of moral

[1] See John Peter, *Complaint and Satire in Early English Literature* (Oxford, 1956), pp. 255–87, which argues strongly for Tourneur as a conscious moralist availing himself of a long established literary tradition, and not as the nihilistic cynic he usually has been called. On *contemptus mundi* and Renaissance pessimism see Herschel Baker, *The Wars of Truth*, pp. 43–50.

exemplum to teach doctrines corollary to a belief in heaven: divine justice, retribution for sinners, the futility of earthly vengeance, and above all the fallacy of any system of human reason which may lead a man to place his faith in physical nature rather than in God.[1]

In Tourneur's tragedies the evil characters outnumber by far the virtuous ones, and their evil is so complete and all-embracing as to leave no room for compensating virtues of any kind; they are shocking in the absoluteness of their depravity. In the same manner such virtuous characters as Castiza or Charlemont are so completely free from sin that they lose all illusion of humanity. It has been suggested[2] that Tourneur was so influenced by current Calvinistic doctrine that he came to see the vast majority of mankind as utterly depraved, with only a few saints who could aspire to heaven. It is obvious that he stresses the world's evil in terms of the gluttony and sexuality for which Puritans had a particular horror, and he does dwell upon the terrors of death which were their constant concern.

But the horror of the body and its pleasures, coupled with a constant concern with death in its most terrible forms, need not be confined to Jacobean Puritanism. These were common features also of medieval asceticism, closely associated with the tradition of *contemptus mundi*. The bitterly satirical portrait of Langebeau Snuffe in *The Atheist's Tragedy* certainly makes it difficult to believe that Tourneur himself could have belonged to any Puritan sect. The rigid division of the characters into good and evil, rather than furnishing evidence of a doctrine of the damned and elect, may simply reflect the rigidity of an allegorical method. Tourneur's characters are never meant to convey the illusion of reality. One like Lussurioso is simply a symbol of lechery, and he contains little which is not a part of this symbol. Castiza or Castabella are symbols of chastity, and they cannot be anything but absolutely virtuous. To find Calvinistic doctrine in Tourneur may also be to

[1] Or, as Miss Ekeblad (*MLR*, LIV (1959), p. 496), sums up the difference between the two plays: 'In "The Atheist's Tragedy" we are asked to follow an argument which eventually proves D'Amville to be wrong and damned; in "The Revenger's Tragedy" we are asked for immediate responses to the evils that are being demonstrated, through the swiftly moving intrigue which hurries us from one striking situation to another, and through out-of-plot speeches.'

[2] Michael H. Higgins, 'The Influence of Calvinistic Thought in Tourneur's "Atheist's Tragedy",' *RES*, XIX (1943), 255–62.

find in his characters a degree of verisimilitude and psychological development which simply is not in them. The enormity of their evil may reflect not a doctrine of man's total depravity so much as the dramatist's desire to shock his audience into belief. He may be relying upon a type of exaggeration which is a common feature of moral *exemplum*. Sin must be writ large.

II

The Revenger's Tragedy is not, as it has so often been regarded, a savage melodrama in which a cynical, embittered adolescent expresses the omnipresence of evil and his own hatred for humanity.[1] The play embodies a distinct moral vision, and this involves more than a belief in the inevitability of divine retribution or in the futility of human vengeance.[2] If the play's action is an ingeniously related series of ironic reversals, these are meaningful only in terms of the larger religious principle which governs the total play: the self-destructive quality of evil and the final insignificance in the light of eternity of man's very life on earth. The scorn for the world which Eliot has called mere adolescent cynicism reflects a profoundly religious view of life, for *The Revenger's Tragedy* is a dramatic statement *de contemptu mundi* which uses the very symbols by which this philosophy of worldly withdrawal and heavenly contemplation had expressed itself in the Middle Ages.[3]

---

[1] See, for instance, A. H. Thorndike, *Tragedy* (Boston, 1905), p. 212; William Archer, *The Old Drama and the New* (London, 1923), p. 74; Una M. Ellis-Fermor, *The Jacobean Drama*, pp. 153–69. For T. S. Eliot, *Selected Essays*, p. 189, the play expresses 'an intense and unique and horrible vision of life; but it is such a vision as might come as the result of few or slender experiences, to a highly sensitive adolescent with a gift for words'. Moody Prior, *The Language of Tragedy*, pp. 135–6, sees the plays as reworkings of the revenge play formula by 'a writer of real poetic gifts who found the most direct release of his talents through the acceptance of a ready-made popular dramatic convention'. For a useful survey of recent criticism, see T. M. Tomlinson, 'The Morality of Revenge: Tourneur's Critics,' *Essays in Criticism*, X (1960), 134–47.

[2] See M. C. Bradbrook, *Theme and Conventions*, pp. 165–74; H. H. Adams, 'Cyril Tourneur on Revenge,' *JEGP*, XLVIII (1949), 72–87; Robert Ornstein, 'The Ethical Design of "The Revenger's Tragedy",' *ELH*, XXI (1954), 81–93, and *The Moral Vision of Jacobean Tragedy*, pp. 107–18.

[3] The medievalism of the play has been stressed by L. G. Salingar, ' "The Revenger's Tragedy" and the Morality Tradition,' *Scrutiny*, VI (1938), 402–22; Ornstein, *The Moral Vision*, p. 117; Schoenbaum, *Middleton's Tragedies*, pp. 28–31.

The medievalism of the play is implicit in its studied artificiality. The characters, with their allegorical names, move across the stage like figures in a medieval dance of death, their actions patterned and ritualistic, until in the final masque scene even the pretence of reality is abandoned. We cannot speak of *The Revenger's Tragedy* in terms of mere survival of an earlier morality play tradition; the play itself is one large dramatic symbol of which the morality play features are an appropriate part, and this total dramatic symbol is medieval both in its grotesqueness and in the view of life for which it provides the emotional equivalent. The unmitigated viciousness of the characters and the unrelieved sinfulness of the action become merely ludicrous when viewed in a naturalistic perspective. Action and character in this play are deliberately unreal, with the exaggerated quality of all symbol, and the theme they emphasize is one of impermanence, change and mutability, the futility of life on earth which renders so urgent a hope in the life beyond. We feel no sorrow at the destruction of Vindice because Tourneur's emphasis is not upon the plight of an individual, or even upon the sorrows of this world, but upon our need to look to the next one.

Such a philosophy of worldly withdrawal does not involve an acquiescence in the face of evil or even an unwilling acceptance of it. It was axiomatic that to merit heaven man must abjure sin in the present world, and thus to preach a doctrine of *contemptu mundi* is implicitly to urge one's fellow men to a life of moral virtue, and this, in effect, is what Tourneur is doing. John Peter has shown that Vindice's speeches draw upon a traditional body of expression whose motive was moral reform, and he has argued that there is in the second half of *The Revenger's Tragedy* a restoration of morality in the world, with a reformation of Gratiana, with Vindice and Hippolito willingly paying the penalty for their own transgressions, and with Castiza and Antonio earning the final victory. The paradox of Tourneur's moral position is that a doctrine of worldly withdrawal may lead at last to social regeneration.

The contrast between a futile earthly vengeance and an effective heavenly justice – heralded by the sound of thunder which answers Vindice's plea (IV, ii) and implicit in the blazing star which hovers

over the final banquet scene (V, iii) – is but part of a larger theme
by which the play is shaped into a unified and consistent work of
art. To this central theme of the impermanence and imperfection
of all human institutions in the light of eternity, all of the parts
of the play contribute. It calls for characters who are symbols of
vanity and waste; it infuses the action with an irony which underscores the futility of all worldly aspirations,[1] and it runs as a leading
motif through the poetic imagery, with its constant playing upon
impermanence, time and change. This central theme is supported
by the unique quality of Tourneur's dramatic verse, whose
rapidity of movement T. S. Eliot has noted (pp. 191–2): 'His
phrases seem to contract the images in his effort to say everything
in the least space, the shortest time.' The total play provides the
emotional equivalent of the statement that life is brief and fleeting,
full of the evil of a corrupt and decaying world, hastening always
towards inevitable death. To seek the things of the world is only
to involve one's self in the evils of the world, to sin, to suffer its
consequences and to die, for man's most careful plans may be
frustrated by fate with a gruesome irony. The only reality worth
man's efforts is the heaven which lies always ahead and which may
be attained by the kind of withdrawal from life and cultivation of
one's own piety which is mirrored in Castiza and Antonio. From
the conviction of heaven's reality springs the sense of reconciliation at the end.

Among the most revealing lines in the play are those with
which Vindice cheerfully accepts his death:

> This murder might have slept in tongueless brass,
> But for ourselves, and the world died an ass;
> Now I remember too, here was Piato
> Brought forth a knavish sentence once;
> No doubt (said he), but time
> Will make the murderer bring forth himself.
>
> (V, iii, 157–61)

The impermanence of human life is contrasted with the permanence of brass, its traditional symbol. Heaven is responsible for

---

[1] On the importance of irony as an instrument of the play's moral argument, see
Peter Lisca, ' "The Revenger's Tragedy": A Study in Irony,' *PQ*, XXXVIII (1959),
242–51.

Vindice's fall, but heaven's instrument is time, which changes all,
reveals all, and reduces life to death: 'Great men were Gods, if
beggars could not kill 'em' (II, ii, 105). This emphasis upon time
and change as the destroyers of life unites the various frustrations
and ironic reversals which constitute the action. It creates a total
impression of the impermanence and futility of earthly existence,
that 'there is nothing sure in mortality, but mortality' (III, vi,
118–19).

The leading motifs of the play are set in Vindice's opening
speech (I, i, 1–52). The skull he holds in his hand is the *memento
mori* which points to the other world, and the evil doers who pass
before him in the torch light are impermanent fragile creatures, of
small significance in the light of eternity. Their very movement
lends them a shadowlike quality and reminds the audience of the
evanescence of human life. In Vindice's words as he watches these
symbols of a debased humanity are the images of time, transmutation, eternal change. The skull is a

> terror to fat folks
> To have their costly three-piled flesh worn off
> As bare as this.

He calls it a 'sallow picture of my poisoned love', the relic of a
beauty that once was. 'Poisoned love' has a double sense, referring
both to the physical poisoning of Gloriana and to the destruction
of his own love which has been changed by poison into hatred and
a lust for revenge. The motif of change is in the thought that
'turns my abused heart-strings into fret'. There is emphasis upon
the passing of time, the instability of nature which kindles fires in
ancient bodies, with the implication also that these are the fires
of hell to which lust leads:

> O that marrowless age,
> Should stuff the hollow bones with damned desires,
> And 'stead of heat kindle infernal fires,
> Within the spendthrift veins of a dry duke,
> A parched and juiceless luxur.

The idea of the transitoriness of life is in 'spendthrift veins', and
even in the image with which Vindice describes the power of his

dead mistress's now vanished beauty there is stress upon change
and transformation, the destruction of human wealth:

> Oh she was able to have made a usurer's son
> Melt all his patrimony in a kiss,
> And what his father fifty years told
> To have consumed.

He calls upon revenge to 'keep thy day, hour, minute' as later he
is to apostrophize, 'O hour of incest!' (I, iii, 70), punctuating the
idea of time and its ravages.

In the imagery of this very speech the audience is reminded also
of heaven, for the eyes of the dead Gloriana, although now trans-
formed to 'those unsightly rings', were once 'two heaven-pointed
diamonds'. The diamond, or crystal, is used throughout the play
as a symbol of heaven and a harmonious cosmic order. When
Vindice would celebrate the virtue of Castiza he calls upon the
angels to give her 'crystal plaudites' (II, i, 267), and she herself
says that 'A virgin honour is a crystal tower' (IV, iv, 165). Castiza
stands for heaven's alternative to the world's corruption and disorder. The diamond is again used as the symbol of a proper moral
order (as opposed to Spurio's bastardy), and the ring as the relic
left when life departs, as the Duchess tries to justify her own
incest:

> thy injury is the more,
> For had he cut thee a right diamond,
> Thou hadst been next set in the dukedom's ring,
> When his worn self like age's easy slave,
> Had dropped out of the collet into th' grave.
> (I, ii, 168–72)

The diamond or crystal of the empyrean was, of course, a traditional symbol for heaven, and the idea of heaven is kept by this
undercurrent of poetic imagery present always in the minds of the
audience. Heaven is in the sound of thunder and in the blazing
star at the end, and it looks down always upon the action:

> Who can perceive this? save that eternal eye
> That sees through flesh and all.
> (I, iii, 74–75)

The action involves not one revenger, but a whole society of revengers.[1] Spurio would avenge himself for his bastardy, the Duchess for her husband's failure to free her youngest son; Ambitioso and Supervacuo seek revenge for their younger brother's death, Lussurioso for his own betrayal. All of these characters are evil, and that they seek revenge makes it inevitable that they be so, for to seek earthly vengeance is implicitly to deny the power and justice of God; it is to involve oneself in the evil of the world. The tragedy of the revenger springs from the failure of his faith in heaven.

Vindice stands somewhat apart from the other avengers because at the beginning of the play the audience is invited to share in the indignation provoked by the wrongs against him, and thus he has their sympathy. He dies, however, as corrupted by sin as the others. He represents the inevitable fate of man who would take upon himself the justice of God, embracing evil in a vain attempt to destroy evil. Vindice is used also to comment on the action, as he does in his opening soliloquy. Once this speech is over he steps directly into the action, assuming three distinct disguises as he manipulates plot and counter plot, his very disguises enforcing the symbolism of impermanence and change.[2]

'What brother,' he asks as he assumes his first disguise, 'am I far enough from myself?' (I, iii, 1) The man who must serve Lussurioso is one 'either disgraced / In former times, or by new grooms displaced' (I, i, 85–86). The human condition is subject to constant flux, and life itself is only 'this luxurious day wherein we breathe' (I, iii, 124). Vindice is described by Hippolito as a symbol of time, the destroyer itself:

> and if time
> Had so much hair, I should take him for time,
> He is so near kin to this present minute.
>
> (I, iii, 27–29)

Vindice becomes the personification of time itself as he catalogues its devastations:

---

[1] H. H. Adams, op. cit., lists nine distinct situations which involve revenge and holds that the play properly should be called *The Revengers' Tragedy*.

[2] On the relation of Vindice's disguises to the morality tradition, see Salingar, op. cit., pp. 409–11.

> I have been witness
> To the surrenders of a thousand virgins,
> And not so little,
> I have seen patrimonies washed a-pieces
> Fruitfields turned into bastards,
> And in a world of acres,
> Not so much dust due to the heir 'twas left to
> As would well gravel a petition!
>
> (I, iii, 54–61)

His rapid changes of person keep pace with the rapid tempo of the action and the verse; they emphasize the relentless passing of time, the instability of the human form, as the things of the world degenerate into dust. Vindice is one 'whose brain time hath seasoned' (II, ii, 8).

The trial of the Duchess's youngest son reveals the inadequacy of human justice, much as Chapman was to dwell upon it in *Chabot*, and through this scene run also the themes of life's impermanence and time's ravages. The Duke in his opening speech calls attention to the power of death to alter the seeming certainties of life:

> Duchess it is your youngest son, we're sorry;
> His violent act has e'en drawn blood of honour
> And stained our honours,
> Thrown ink upon the forehead of our state
> Which envious spirits will dip their pens into
> After our death, and blot us in our tombs.
> For that which would seem treason in our lives
> Is laughter when we're dead.
>
> (I, ii, 1–8)

Blood has not even the durability and power of ink, which at least can survive to destroy reputation and honour after death has triumphed. The theme of transmutation is echoed by Spurio: 'Would all the court were turned into a corpse' (I, ii, 40), and the bizarre metaphor of blood and ink is later recalled in 'The pen of his bastard writes him cuckold' (II, ii, 121), with its additional sexual connotation, the reputation of the Duke himself being destroyed by the very power of ink he now decries.

Throughout the play the human body is described as a building, subject to ruin and decay. The murdered wife of Antonio is called 'a fair comely building new fallen, / Being falsely undermined' (I, iv, 72). This building imagery is used also to emphasize the impermanence of life and the futility of all worldly aspirations, and this motif is given an ironic emphasis when the evil Lussurioso uses this very imagery to boast of his power to make the fortunes of men:

> For thy sake we'll advance him, and build fair
> His meanest fortunes; for it is in us
> To rear up towers from cottages.
>
> (IV, i, 61–63)

When the condemned Junior speaks of the beauty of Antonio's wife as 'ordained to be my scaffold' (I, ii, 71), there may be a double implication in 'scaffold', a temporary building as well as the gallows, but whether this be intentional or not, the line focuses upon the relation of beauty to death which is so integral to the theme of the play.

This theme appears most markedly on Vindice's second appearance with the skull of Gloriana. His speech is a virtual catalogue of the medieval commonplaces *de contemptu mundi*. There is scorn for the love of woman as futile worship of what must inevitably degenerate into dust:

> And now methinks I could e'en chide myself,
> For doting on her beauty.
>
> (III, v, 72–73)

The impermanence of physical beauty and the futility of its worship are expressed in perhaps the best known lines in the play:

> Does the silkworm expend her yellow labours
> For thee? for thee does she undo herself?
> Are lordships sold to maintain ladyships
> For the poor benefit of a bewitching minute?
>
> (75–78)

As the silkworm gives his body, man gives his soul to glorify lechery and whoredom. 'Ladyship' was sometimes used for bawd, and the soul was often called the lord of the body. Life is only a 'bewitching minute' and beauty leads only to damnation. The very act of preserving beauty is identified poetically with the destruction of human life:

> Does every proud and self-affecting dame
> Camphor her face for this? and grieve her Maker
> In sinful baths of milk, — when many an infant starves,
> For her superfluous outside, all for this?
>
> (87–90)

The skull is the only reality. It is the medieval *memento mori* whose presence at the feast would banish thoughts of worldly vanity and turn man to contemplation of the world to come:

> it were fine methinks,
> To have thee seen at revels, forgetful feasts,
> And unclean brothels; sure 'twould fright the sinner
> And make him a good coward, put a reveller
> Out of his antic amble
> And cloy an epicure with empty dishes.
> Here might a scornful and ambitious woman
> Look through and through herself, — see ladies, with
>   false forms
> You deceive men, but cannot deceive worms.
>
> (93–101)

Vindice turns to the audience with his 'see ladies', the author speaking directly. In the symbol of the skull are all of its traditional associations.[1]

Castiza, the symbol of a heavenly order whose mark is chastity, stands apart from the other characters. She represents the permanence of heavenly virtue as opposed to the transitory everchanging life of sin which the other characters exemplify. She is 'a rare phoenix' (I, iii, 111), for virtue alone is eternal, and her very first speech underscores the motifs of constancy and poverty which are the signs of virtue. Her poverty is an implicit rejection of the evanescent things of the world:

> How hardly shall that maiden be beset,
> Whose only fortunes are her constant thoughts,
> That has no other child's part but her honour,
> That keeps her low and empty in estate.
>
> (II, i, 1–4)

---

[1] On the traditional nature of Vindice's speech and its relation to the religious complaint, see Peter, *Complaint and Satire*, pp. 262–4.

This symbol of constancy is necessary to the total design of the play, for it reminds the audience of the heaven where alone this constancy can exist. By her rejection of the world Castiza stands for heaven, and it is the reality of heaven which makes meaningful the scorn for the world which the total play espouses. Castiza provides a frame of reference for the moral argument of the play.

The constancy of Castiza throws into relief the inconstancy of her mother, the sudden collapse of a seeming virtue:

> I cry you mercy. Lady, I mistook you,
> Pray did you see my mother; which way went you?
> Pray God I have not lost her.
>
> (II, i, 180–3)

This wavering of Gratiana, departure from herself, repeats the motif of the rapid changes in the person of Vindice. Castiza drives home the theme:

> The world's so changed, one shape into another,
> It is a wise child now that knows her mother.
>
> (II, i, 187–8)

In urging her daughter to sin Gratiana dwells on the theme of time. She urges Castiza to 'understand your time' (II, i, 193), echoing Vindice's earlier placing of sin in terms of the clock:

> If anything be damned,
> It will be twelve a clock at night; that twelve
> Will never 'scape;
> It is the Judas of the hours, wherein,
> Honest salvation is betrayed to sin.
>
> (I, iii, 75–79)

His fee for pandering will be 'all the farthingales that fall plump about twelve a clock at night upon the rushes' (II, ii, 91–92). The Duke will meet his death when he goes to indulge his lust 'in this unsunned lodge, / Wherein 'tis night at noon' (III, v, 20–21).

Each of the play's sub-plots involves an ironic reversal which illustrates the futility of worldly plans. These are united to one another and to the main plot not only by this common irony, but by a similar poetic idiom which in the undercurrent of its imagery emphasizes always the destructive power of an ever hastening time. As Vindice tempts Castiza with the worldly pleasures of the court, the tempo of his lines quickens, conveying the sense of rapid movement and perpetual change:

> O think upon the pleasure of the palace,
> Secured ease and state; the stirring meats,
> Ready to move out of the dishes, that e'en now
> Quicken when they're eaten,
> Banquets abroad by torchlight, music, sports,
> Bareheaded vassals, that had ne'er the fortune
> To keep on their own hats, but let horns wear 'em.
> Nine coaches waiting – hurry, hurry, hurry.
>
> (II, i, 223–9)

The way of the world is symbolized by movement, haste, speeding minutes, perpetual change. To tempt Castiza, Vindice must 'set spurs to the mother' (II, ii, 53), for 'a right good woman in these days is changed / Into white money with less labour far' (II, ii, 31–32). But the way of Castiza is not that of perishing mortality, but of heaven's permanence. Even with his 'golden spurs' Vindice cannot 'put her to a false gallop in a trice' (II, ii, 53–54).

Similarly, in the Junior sub-plot, Tourneur creates the feeling of furious haste as Junior is led to his execution, with the First Officer's 'So suddenly' (III, iii, 11), the Second Officer's 'Already?' (III, iii, 15), its repetition by Supervacuo, 'Already i' faith, O sir, destruction hies' (III, iii, 116), and his final reflection that his brother must die 'ere next clock' (III, iii, 36). 'There's no delaying time' (III, iv, 49), says the Third Officer as he leads Junior to his death, repeating a major theme of the play. It is implicit in the ironic predicament of Vindice when he is commissioned to kill himself, for to live is to kill one's self with the passing of time, and this Vindice does.

'Now nine years' vengeance crowd into a minute' (III, v, 126), cries Vindice as he prepares with Hippolito for the Duke's murder. The grim irony by which they bring about their own destructions is paralleled by the lesser ironies of the play: those of Spurio's incestuous relations with the Duchess, Lussurioso's attempt to thwart this affair, the counter plots of Ambitioso and Supervacuo, with the resulting death of their younger brother. Through all this action run the motifs of time and change. Spurio will disinherit

Lussurioso in 'as short time, / As I was when I was begot in haste' (II, ii, 141–2). 'This night, this hour – this minute, now' (II, ii, 183), cries Vindice as he rushes Lussurioso to his father's bedchamber, and this is echoed in the Duke's plea for his life: 'I must have days, / Nay months dear son' (II, ii, 215–16). Spurio runs into his father's chamber with 'is the day out at socket, / That it is noon at midnight'? (II, ii, 257–8).

Tourneur designed the world of *The Revenger's Tragedy* to represent the ordinary world of sinful man which is merely a brief interval before eternity. This sense of ordinary life is borne out also by the poetic imagery, particularly that drawn from the common occupations of everyday life, from building and business exchange, from domestic life, farming and gardening. The feeling that this world is hasting to its end is conveyed not only by the constant stress on time, change and speed but also by the metaphors of fire which are so common in the play. The macabre grotesqueness of the action contributes to a larger moral vision which cannot be perceived in naturalistic terms, for the play is a symbolic work of art in the medieval mode, and to enforce its symbolism it uses a kind of exaggeration and distortion which is alien to a naturalistic dramatic method. The horrors of the action cannot be viewed outside their context as part of a larger religious symbol. Tourneur's audience would leave the theatre not so much with a sense of cynicism or despair as with that particular sense of the imperfection and impermanence of worldly things which leads naturally to contemplation of the perfect life to come.

III

There are two parallel movements in *The Atheist's Tragedy*, the one devoted to a systematic refutation of the reason of D'Amville which has led him to atheism, and the other designed to demonstrate the power of the true believer to overcome evil by Christian patience and, with the help of God, to triumph over the forces which oppress him. These two movements are skilfully united in the opposition between D'Amville and Charlemont, the evil persecutor and his seemingly helpless victim, and both of Tourneur's main points are made by the final axe stroke which knocks out D'Amville's brains, not to be regarded as a ludicrous accident by which a child-like dramatist resolves his plot, but rather as a miracle, deliberately chosen for its apparent impossibility, by which Tourneur emphasizes the intervention of God to destroy the wicked and protect the innocent.

D'Amville is not merely a disbeliever in God. Atheism in the Renaissance had a positive as well as a negative aspect. He is a worshipper of nature, which he considers as a self-sufficient entity, governed by laws which man can understand by the power of reason, and subject to no supernatural control. He believes that by his own human will and the power of his mind he can manipulate the world and other men to his own advantage. He stands, like Shakespeare's Edmund, for Renaissance scepticism, and his creation reflects the fear and horror with which conservative minds viewed the growth of a new empirical science and the challenging of traditional values of order and degree. It has been shown that D'Amville is a perfect example of what the Renaissance called atheism, that he was systematically created from notions about atheism which appeared in contemporary writings, and that a cardinal feature of such atheistic belief was to regard nature's laws as running contrary to the laws of God.[1]

Since he recognizes no supernatural power in the universe, the atheist can know none of those feelings of love, loyalty, kindness, gratitude and the like which Renaissance moralists held to be emanations on the human plane of the love of God which rules the universe. The atheist must by virtual definition be an absolute villain, knowing no restrictions to the gratification of his own sensual appetite. The goal of man he sees not as salvation, but only as pleasure, profit, and power. D'Amville's philosophy is made clear in the opening scene of the play in his conversation with Borachio. It begins with an equation of man and beast, for to deny the presence of heaven is implicitly to deny also that spiritual quality which man derives from heaven and which separates him from the beast:

[1] Robert Ornstein, ' "The Atheist's Tragedy" and Renaissance Naturalism,' *SP*, LI (1954), 194–207. Ornstein holds that D'Amville's view of nature is never refuted in the play, and that Tourneur therefore accepts a dichotomy between natural law and moral law. But the point of the entire play is to refute D'Amville's position. See also *The Moral Vision*, pp. 118–27.

> *D'Am.* Borachio, thou art read
>   In nature and her large philosophy.
>   Observ'st thou not the very selfsame course
>   Of revolution both in man and beast?
>
> *Bor.*   The same. For birth, growth, state, decay
>   and death:
>   Only a man's beholding to his nature
>   For th'better composition of the two.
>
>   (I, i, 4–10)

It is only the quality of his own physical composition which renders man superior to the beasts in this view, and when this 'nature' is defective in any way man becomes like any beast:

> But where the favour of his nature is
> Not full and free; you see a man becomes
> A fool, as little knowing as a beast.
>
>   (I, i, 11–13)

This self sufficiency of the human animal is an implicit denial of God's existence:

> That shows there's nothing in a man, above
> His nature; if there were, considering 'tis
> His being's excellency, 'twould not yield
> To nature's weakness.
>
>   (I, i, 14–17)

And if there is no God or afterlife, man must spend his little time on earth in pursuit of pleasure:

> Then if death casts up
> Our total sum of joy and happiness;
> Let me have all my senses feasted in
> Th'abundant fullness of delight at once,
> And with a sweet insensible increase
> Of pleasing surfeit melt into my dust.
>
>   (I, i, 18–25)

D'Amville even deludes himself that the man of reason can escape the final fact of human mortality, that through his children he can live forever, and thus retain the wealth which has been the sole mark of his felicity, and to whose pursuit his life has been devoted:

Yet even in that sufficiency of state,
A man has reason to provide and add.
For what is he hath such a present eye,
And so prepared a strength, that can foresee,
And fortify his substance and himself,
Against those accidents, the least whereof
May rob him of an age's husbandry?
And for my children; they are as near to me,
As branches to the tree whereon they grow,
And may as numerously be multiplied.
As they increase, so should my providence;
For from my substance they receive the sap,
Whereby they live and flourish.

(I, i, 52–64)

In this expectation the audience sees already the extent of the atheist's delusion, for he has placed his hope in sons whose mortality is as fragile as his own, the one subject to physical disease and the other to lechery which will destroy him.

In its forthright didacticism the play carries on many features of the medieval *débat*. D'Amville proclaims his nature philosophy directly to the audience, both in soliloquies and in discussions with Borachio which show also the influence of the Senecan dialogue. Charlemont and Castabella proclaim in the same manner the virtues of Christian patience, chastity and submission to divine will. By these beliefs they are preserved, whereas all of D'Amville's plots rebound upon himself. By ironic reversals similar to those of *The Revenger's Tragedy*, we are reminded that as the atheist tries to destroy the virtuous he succeeds only in destroying himself. D'Amville and Borachio pride themselves always upon their cunning; they gloat over their machinations, so that the final disaster which overtakes them may demonstrate also that their cunning has, in fact, been gross stupidity, and that the 'reason' by which D'Amville has lived and which has led him to embrace atheism has been only a self-deception and not reason at all. He has relied upon his 'strength of natural understanding', but he learns at the end that 'Nature is a fool. There is a power / Above her that hath overthrown the pride / Of all my projects and posterity' (V, ii, 282–6).

We have thus in the conflict between the good and evil

characters a debate between two opposing systems of value, with orthodox Christianity triumphant at the end and D'Amville learning the lesson of his defeat. One facet of this debate is the conflict between chastity and lust which runs through the play and is reflected largely in the opposition of Castabella to Levidulcia. For Castabella, as her name implies, love is chastity:

> O love! thou chaste affection of the soul,
> Without th'adulterate mixture of the blood;
> That virtue which to goodness addeth good,
> The minion of heaven's heart.
>
> (II, iii, 1–4)

Levidulcia, like D'Amville, denies the difference between man and beast; she is the slave of an animal passion over which she can have no control:

> My strange affection to this man! — 'Tis like that natural sympathy which e'en among the senseless creatures of the earth commands a mutual inclination and consent: For though it seems to be the free effect of mine own voluntary love; yet I can neither restrain it, nor give reason for't.
>
> (IV, v, 15–19)

Those who accept the animalism of man see him as controlled by the mechanical laws of nature; he is the pawn of a fate uncontrolled by divine providence, as D'Amville states it:

> And I am of a confident belief,
> That even the time, place, manner of our deaths,
> Do follow fate with that necessity
> That makes us sure to die. And in a thing
> Ordained so certainly unalterable,
> What can the use of providence prevail?
>
> (I, ii, 48–53)

D'Amville, in his defence of incest, envies the brute animals who know no restrictions in their pleasures:

> Nature allows a general liberty
> Of generation to all creatures else.
> Shall man to whose command and use all creatures

Were made subject be less free than they?

(IV, iii, 143–6)

To this argument Castabella offers Tourneur's answer:

> O God! is thy unlimited and infinite
> Omnipotence less free because thou doest
> No ill? or if you argue merely out
> Of nature, do you not degenerate
> From that; and are you not unworthy the
> Prerogative of nature's masterpiece,
> When basely you prescribe yourself
> Authority and law from their examples
> Whom you should command.

(IV, iii, 147–55)

Just as D'Amville sees man as an animal governed only by the laws of an impersonal nature, with worldly pleasure and power his only goals in life, Charlemont sees man as a creature of spirit, controlled by a just and omnipotent deity to whom he is always subject. Charlemont is the 'Senecal Man'[1] who is always master of his own passions:

> But now I am an emperor of a world,
> This little world of man. My passions are
> My subjects; and I can command them laugh;
> Whilst thou dost tickle 'em to death with misery.

(III, iii, 46–49)

His universe is a divinely ordered one where heaven 'doth command / Our punishments: but yet no further than / The measure of our sins' (III, iii, 1–3). He is, in short, a model of Christian patience who submits freely to the pain and misery of life, confident always in the perfection of God's plan, ready to accept whatever misfortune comes his way in the assurance that good must at last triumph. He reflects the kind of virtue which the horrors of *The Revenger's Tragedy* were designed to teach. His eyes are always on the afterworld, and he even thanks heaven for his misfortunes when out of them he sees his final happiness emerging:

[1] See Michael Higgins, 'The Development of the Senecal Man,' *RES*, XXIII (1947), 24–33; Clifford Leech, ' "The Atheist's Tragedy" as a Dramatic Comment on Chapman's *Bussy* plays,' *JEGP*, LIII (1953), 525–30.

> For all my wrongs I thank thee gracious heaven;
> Th'ast made satisfaction, to reserve
> Me for this blessed purpose. Now sweet death,
> I'll bid thee welcome.

> (IV, iii, 198–201)

In his readiness for death he expresses directly the attitude *de contemptu mundi* which *The Revenger's Tragedy* had in its totality espoused:

> That man, with so much labour should aspire
> To worldly height; when in the humble earth,
> The world's condition's at the best! Or scorn
> Inferior men; since to be lower than
> A worm is to be higher than a king.

> (IV, iii, 19–23)

Charlemont's Christian patience appears particularly in his attitude towards revenge which is a major theme of the play. When the ghost of his father appears to tell Charlemont of his murder, he counsels Christian submission:

> Attend with patience the success of things;
> But leave revenge unto the king of kings.
> (II, vi, 26–27)

And again, when Charlemont has stabbed Sebastian, his father's ghost appears to warn him:

> Hold, Charlemont.
> Let him revenge my murder, and thy wrongs
> To whom the justice of revenge belongs.
> (III, ii, 43–45)

Charlemont is torn 'between the passions of / My blood and the religion of my soul' (III, ii, 46–47), but he nevertheless accepts his father's injunction and never wavers from it. He never seeks to raise his hand against his persecutor, and he patiently places his head upon the block, unafraid to die because his faith in heavenly justice has never wavered. When heaven acts at last and intervenes to destroy D'Amville and to spare Charlemont's life, he speaks the moral for the audience:

Only to heaven I attribute the work.
Whose gracious motives made me still forbear
To be mine own revenger. Now I see,
That, *Patience is the honest man's revenge.*

(V, ii, 300–04)

Because he is an atheist the destruction of D'Amville is inevitable, but we must note that in spite of his damnation he is no longer an atheist when he dies. He learns the lesson of his own destruction and comes to recognize the power of divine providence at last. As his plans begin to backfire we note a wavering in his confidence in nature, a gradual questioning of his once strongly held beliefs, until at the end he is ready to renounce them entirely.

There is a gross macabre humour in the graveyard scenes, but these scenes mark also the beginning of D'Amville's conversion. He is terrified by the signs of death and begins 'to feel the loathsome horror of my sin' (IV, iii, 52–53). Contrasted with his terror of death is Charlemont's fearless acceptance of it, and the realization of his own weakness in this respect causes the atheist to doubt the validity of his own beliefs. When he sees Charlemont and Castabella sleeping peacefully upon their death's head pillows, he has a vision of a kind of felicity to which his own 'reason' is incapable of leading him:

Asleep? so soundly? and so sweetly upon death's heads? and in a place so full of fear and horror? Sure there is some other happiness within the freedom of the conscience, than my knowledge e'er attained to.

(IV, iii, 316–19)

When he sees his own hope of immortality finally destroyed in the deaths of his two sons, D'Amville recognizes the inadequacy of his faith in nature, and for the first time he acknowledges a supernatural power: 'Sure there is some power above her that controls her force' (V, i, 126–7). The doctor is left to affirm for D'Amville and the audience the play's refutation of the atheist position:

A power above Nature?
Doubt you that my lord? Consider but
Whence man receives his body and his form.

> Not from corruption like some worms and flies;
> But only from the generation of
> A man. For nature never did bring forth
> A man without a man; nor could the first
> Man being but the passive subject not
> The active mover, be the maker of
> Himself; So of necessity there must
> Be a superior power to nature.
>
>   (V, i, 128–38)

Such straightforward statement of the play's moral argument was hardly necessary in *The Revenger's Tragedy*, where it was conveyed instead by the total complex of the dramatic action.

The court scene with which the play ends serves as a symbolic reaffirmation of order. D'Amville's position is systematically refuted, and the joyful rescue of Charlemont and Castabella is offered as evidence of the heavenly power which the atheist had denied. Cataplasma, Soquette and Fresco receive the punishment their vice has merited, and the Puritan whose religious hypocrisy D'Amville had used as an argument against all religion (I, ii, 218–23) is unmasked as Snuffe the tallow chandler and sent on his way. Then the judge is ready to 'resolve your question' (V, ii, 108), teach D'Amville what it is which enables Charlemont to face death without fear. The atheist now must 'find out / The efficient cause of a contented mind' (V, ii, 184).

Charlemont and Castabella can die bravely because they have their virtue to sustain them:

>   Our lives cut off,
> In our young prime of years, are like green herbs,
> Wherewith we strow the hearses of our friends.
> For as their virtue gather'd when th'are green,
> Before they wither or corrupt, is best;
> So we in virtue are the best for death,
> While yet we have not lived to such an age,
> That the increasing canker of our sins,
> Hath spread too far upon us.
>
>   (V, ii, 145–53)

Castabella is welcoming death as a means of escape from that involvement in sin which is the inevitable consequence of living, and which the fate of Vindice in *The Revenger's Tragedy* had so well illustrated. To die young is to die with the maximum of virtue, and such virtue is a greater good than life, for through it man may attain heaven. These chaste lovers can die bravely because of a contempt for the world and all its impermanent and corrupting values. They reveal to the atheist the final worthlessness of the worldly pleasure, wealth, and power which have been the goals of his existence.

D'Amville receives a further answer to his own question with the very blow with which he strikes out his brains, for this miraculous accident is evidence of the divine providence in which Charlemont and Castabella have placed their faith and which also has given them courage in the face of death. In the justice of his own death through divine intervention D'Amville recognizes the power of providence:

> But yond' power that struck me knew
> The judgment I deserved; and gave it.
>
> > (V, ii, 290-1)

Again the point is emphasized for the audience by the judge as he points to the new felicity of Charlemont and Castabella:

> With the hands
> Of joy and justice I thus set you free.
> The power of that eternal providence,
> Which overthrew his projects in their pride,
> Hath made your griefs the instruments to raise
> Your blessings to a greater height than ever.
>
> > (V, ii, 294-9)

Out of man's very ability to suffer the world's evil with Christian patience must emerge his final blessings, and it is significant that the consistent virtue of Charlemont and Castabella assures their happiness not only in heaven but in the present world as well. Charlemont is Tourneur's answer to the question of how a good man may live in a world corrupted by the reality of sin and death. It is an answer in terms of a traditional Christianity, and it is essentially the same answer which Tourneur had offered in a somewhat different poetic medium in *The Revenger's Tragedy*. The second of Tourneur's tragedies exhibits little progress in aesthetic range, but it is remarkably like the earlier one in its moral and religious point of view.

CHAPTER FIVE

John Webster

I

When we consider John Webster's achievement as a dramatist we are struck by a general mediocrity, suddenly relieved in the middle of his career by two plays, written in quick succession, of a brilliance and power virtually unequalled in his age. *The White Devil* and *The Duchess of Malfi* were composed in 1612 and 1613, following a period of uninspired collaboration with Dekker, Heywood and others; they were followed by some further independent work and by renewed collaboration with Middleton, Heywood and Rowley, but never again, working either alone or with others, did Webster approach the aesthetic range of his two Italian tragedies. They seem to represent the artist's concentrated attempt to express a tragic vision which he imperfectly perceived in *The White Devil*, and realized fully in *The Duchess of Malfi*, after which his career could only culminate in anti-climax. He had nothing more to say.

Webster's plays often have been compared to Tourneur's, largely because both dramatists avail themselves of the neo-Senecan horror devices made popular by John Marston, but there is a difference between the two men which is far greater than any similarity. Tourneur, as we have seen, is the explicit moralist, preaching in effect an orthodox Christianity to which he is firmly committed. Webster is no less the moralist, but he does not preach. His plays are an agonized search for moral order in the uncertain and chaotic world of Jacobean scepticism by a dramatist who can no longer accept without question the postulates of order and degree so dear to the Elizabethans. In *The White Devil* Webster creates a poetic impression of this world with its inherent contradictions, but he can find in his story no pattern to relate good and evil and provide a basis for morality. In the heroic death of his heroine, her preservation even in evil of her 'integrity of life', however, he is able to excite admiration and thus to leave his audience with the impression that there is at least one certain value, if attainable only in death, in a world seemingly without value. In *The Duchess of Malfi* Webster goes on to explore the implications of this value. If death may reveal an inherent nobility in human life, such nobility is real, and it may be the basis of a moral order. In *The Duchess of Malfi* we see a new morality emerging in the final act out of evils more chilling in their horror than those of the earlier play. This search for moral order links Webster to Shakespeare in the highest range of tragedy, and to fully perceive Webster's achievement we must see his later play as the exploration of a value postulated in the earlier one and as the final resolution of the problem with which both plays are concerned.

The Italian tragedies have been celebrated for their unity of tone and temper, for their realism of characterization in spite of a glaring weakness in psychological motivation, and for the brilliance of their dramatic verse. They have been criticized for their plot construction, with its gross improbabilities, and for a concern with 'perfection of detail rather than general design'[1] which has made it difficult for most critics to find even in these greatest of Webster's plays such thematic unity as may be found, for instance, in the tragedies of Chapman or Tourneur. T. S. Eliot has called Webster 'a very great literary and dramatic genius directed toward chaos',[2] and Clifford Leech expresses a common judgment when he writes that *The Duchess of Malfi* 'is blurred in its total meaning. It is a collection of brilliant scenes, whose statements do not ultimately cohere'.[3] The final act of this play has been called an unnecessary and anti-climactic extension of what should have ended with the death of the heroine.[4]

---

[1] M. C. Bradbrook, *Themes and Conventions of Elizabethan Tragedy*, p. 186 ff.

[2] *Selected Essays*, p. 117.

[3] *John Webster* (London, 1951), p. 65. So also, Travis Bogard, *The Tragic Satire of John Webster* (Berkeley, Calif., 1955), p. 117, writes that Webster was 'apparently unable to discover an acceptable system for the evaluation of good and evil', and concludes that ' "The White Devil" is a tragedy of disillusion, "The Duchess of Malfi" a tragedy of despair' (p. 141).

[4] F. L. Lucas, ed. *The Duchess of Malfi* (London, 1958), pp. 28–35.

We do no justice to Webster's achievement in these plays while, like Lucas, we regard the dramatist as a naturalistic artist, following sordid historical narratives for their own sake, the sum of his greatness being in 'atmosphere, its poetry, and two or three supreme scenes'.[1] These plays, like the greatest tragedies of their age, have an ethical and an allegorical dimension. They are symbolic works, and if their poetry is great it is because of its perfection as the instrument by which the artist reveals a vision of man's relation to the forces of evil in the world and affords a basis for renewed acceptance of life which is tragic reconciliation. The most serious error that critics of Webster have committed has been to regard him as a dramatist lacking in moral vision, and therefore incapable of more than a partial view of human experience, content to limit his genius within the bounds of a philosophically barren tradition of revenge tragedy.[2]

In *The White Devil* Webster is concerned with the deception of appearances, the unreality of the world in which man must live, and with the shallowness of the conventional moral order. The play is a dramatic symbol of moral confusion, the impossibility of distinguishing appearance from reality in a world in which evil wears always the mask of virtue and virtue the mask of evil.[3]

[1] *The Duchess of Malfi*, p. 31. Webster's weakness in structure is stressed also by Ornstein, *The Moral Vision of Jacobean Tragedy*, pp. 128-31.

[2] Ian Jack, 'The Case of John Webster,' *Scrutiny*, XVI (1949), 38-43, has found Webster's art deficient because 'There is no correspondence between the axioms and the life represented in the drama'. Essentially the same point is made by Ornstein, *The Moral Vision*, pp. 128-50, although he sees in *The Duchess of Malfi* a movement away from 'the lack of moral discriminations in "The White Devil" towards a more consistent moral view of life, a celebration of the power of illusion to assure some victory for mankind in an evil world. That Webster is a dramatist without moral vision, capable of only a meaningless sensationalism, has been argued also by W. R. Edwards, 'John Webster,' in *Determinations*, ed. F. R. Leavis (London, 1934), pp. 155-78. The morality of Webster's art, on the contrary, has been argued by Lord David Cecil, *Poets and Storytellers* (London, 1949), pp. 27-43. Cecil tries to find Webster's morality in terms of a Calvinistic Christianity.

[3] See Hereward T. Price, 'The Function of Imagery in Webster,' *PMLA*, LXX (1955), 717-39; John Russell Brown, ed., *The White Devil* (London, 1960), pp. l-lviii. It has been argued also that in *The White Devil* Vittoria achieves nobility by her ability to assume the mask of a virtue she does not possess, and that in this she is offered as contrast to the open villainy of Flamineo, the two positions balancing one another in a kind of equilibrium out of which no moral certainty can emerge. See B. J. Laymon, 'The Equilibrium of Opposites in "The White Devil": A Reinterpretation,' *PMLA*, LXXIV (1959), 336-47.

In this world morality seems impossible, but in *The Duchess of Malfi* Webster reveals how it may be possible in spite of this world. Webster's cosmic view is not the optimistic one of Hooker, Shakespeare or Heywood. His is the decaying universe of Chapman and Tourneur, hastening towards destruction. Although there are references to heaven and hell in his plays, Webster's world is 'a mist' without order or design, and with no certainty of a divine providence directing the affairs of men. The two plays taken together, however, do not reveal a philosophy of negation or despair,[1] for Webster's concern is with the ability of man to survive in such a world without direction, to maintain his human worth in spite of all. This is a profoundly moral concern, for morality need not be based upon faith in divine order. Webster bases his faith upon human integrity and in the nobility to which human life can aspire in spite of the disorder which surrounds it.

II

Deception and false appearance are accented both in the dramatic action and the poetic imagery of *The White Devil*. Evil wears always the mask of good, and good disguises itself as evil, so that at last the two are indistinguishable. This moral ambiguity is implicit in the play's title, and it is maintained by an imagery comprised of polar opposites: 'Sweet-meats which rot the eater . . . Poison'd perfumes . . . Shipwrecks in calmest weather' (III, ii, 80–82). False appearance is introduced in the first speech of the play: 'Your wolf no longer seems to be a wolf / Than when she's hungry' (I, i, 8–9). The garden where the lovers meet becomes a graveyard:

> O that this fair garden
> Had with all poisoned herbs of Thessaly
> At first been planted, made a nursery
> For witchcraft; rather than a burial plot,
> For both your honours.

(I, ii, 274–8)

[1] Thus, for Una M. Ellis-Fermor, *The Jacobean Drama*, pp. 172–3, Webster's chief concern is to stress the unreality of a bleak and meaningless universe: 'this negation, the quality of nothingness, this empty, boundless, indefinable grey mist is the final horror, the symbol of ignorance, of the infinite empty space in which man hovers, the material and the spiritual world both in different terms unreal.'

The dovehouse is haunted by polecats (II, i, 3–5). Vittoria herself, the symbol of this confusion, is compared to the apples of Sodom which turn to soot and ashes when they are tasted (III, ii, 63–67). A recurring symbol is that of the yew tree, whose beauty and fair height are rooted in corruption:

> Or like the black, and melancholic yew tree,
> Dost think to root thyself in dead men's graves,
> And yet to prosper?
>
> (IV, iii, 120–2)

Vittoria's dream of the yew tree (I, ii, 231 ff.) leads Bracciano to the murders of Isabella and Camillo. Beauty is the product of disease and decay, and this beauty is in turn the destroyer of life, the creator of new disease in an endless cycle. Vittoria's beauty, shining through her evil, is the symbol of this meaningless, uncertain condition of humanity.

When she is guilty of her greatest sins, she is most able to arouse the admiration of the audience by her defiance and heroic grandeur:

> Humbly thus,
> Thus low, to the most worthy and respected
> Lieger Ambassadors, my modesty
> And womanhood I tender; but withal
> So entangled in a cursed accusation
> That my defence of force like Perseus,
> Must personate masculine virtue – to the point!
> Find me but guilty, sever head from body:
> We'll part good friends: I scorn to hold my life
> At yours or any man's entreaty, Sir.
>
> (III, ii, 130–9)

We do not doubt her 'modesty and womanhood' here; Webster uses the English ambassador to guide the sentiments of his audience: 'She hath a brave spirit' (III, ii, 140). But while we admire Vittoria we know that she lies, and the Cardinal in pointing to her falsehood, underlines the confusion of appearance with reality for which she stands: 'Well, well, such counterfeit jewels / Make true ones oft suspected' (III, ii, 141–2).

Vittoria's defiance is a dramatic symbol of this moral confusion, for in the vehemence of her speech she turns her own evil back upon her judges, so that there is no difference between accusers and accused:

> You are deceived;
> For know that all your strict-combined heads,
> Which strike against this mine of diamonds,
> Shall prove but glassen hammers, they shall break, –
> These are but feigned shadows of my evils.
> Terrify babes, my lord, with painted devils,
> I am past such needless palsy, – for your names
> Of whore and murd'ress, they proceed from you,
> As if a man should spit against the wind,
> The filth returns in's face.
>
> (III, ii, 142–51)

The audience has seen Vittoria's evil made explicit in action. Now it is caught up in the splendour and vehemence of her passionate denial, and it is left in a state of ambivalence. If the morality she opposes is represented by the Cardinal Monticelso, this morality is indeed a 'glassen hammer' and she a 'mine of diamonds'; she may be a whore, but the Cardinal has 'ravish'd justice, / Forc'd her to do your pleasure' (III, ii, 274–5). She leaves the scene condemned but triumphant, and her final words reflect the paradox of the play: 'Through darkness diamonds spread their richest light' (III, ii, 294).

Our sense of moral ambivalence is reinforced when we find the Cardinal, Vittoria's judge, as the author of the Machiavellian deception by which Francesco de Medici will accomplish his revenge (IV, i, 14 ff.). In the Cardinal's book lurk all the evils of the world, a catalogue of villainies robed in seeming virtue:

> Their number rises strangely,
> And some of them
> You'd take for honest men.
> Next are pandars.
> These are your pirates: and these following leaves
> For base rogues that undo young gentlemen
> By taking up commodities:
> For politic bankrupts:
> For fellows that are bawds to their own wives,
> Only to put off horses and slight jewels,
> Clocks, defac'd plate, and such commodities,

At birth of their first children . . .
These are for impudent bawds,
That go in men's apparel: for usurers
That share with scriveners for their good reportage:
For lawyers that will antedate their writs:
And some divines you might find folded there,
But that I slip them o'er for conscience' sake.
Here is a general catalogue of knaves.
A man might study all the prisons o'er,
Yet never attain this knowledge.

                              (IV, ii, 45–64)

Religion is the source of policy, and this policy Francesco will use to destroy Vittoria. The Cardinal's judging of Vittoria becomes a mockery of justice, his very existence an implicit denial of the traditional morality of which his title makes him the symbol.

There are virtuous characters in *The White Devil*, Cornelia, Isabella, Marcello, but real as their virtue may be, it appears to the world cloaked in evil. Isabella's love for Bracciano must express itself in her pretence that she is the evil destroyer of their marriage:

                         let the fault
        Remain with my supposed jealousy, –
        And think with what a piteous and rent heart,
        I shall perform this sad ensuing part.

                              (II, i, 222–5)

Her 'piteous and rent heart' will appear to the world as evil; her brother will call her 'a foolish, mad, / And jealous woman' (II, i, 264–5). In the same manner, the maternal love of Cornelia expresses itself in her lies to protect the murderer of the very son she mourns. Marcello sees his death as just punishment for the evils of his family:

        There are some sins which heaven doth duly punish
        In a whole family. This it is to rise
        By all dishonest means. Let all men know
        That tree shall long time keep a steady foot
        Whose branches spread no wider than the root.

                              (V, ii, 20–24)

He cannot escape the evil from which he springs. Even the young Giovanni, attempting to restore order at the end of the play, is

closely related to the very evils he seeks to destroy, for he is the
son of Bracciano, and when he asks, 'You bloody villains, / By
what authority have you committed / This massacre?' the answer
is 'By thine . . . Yes, thy uncle, / Which is a part of thee, enjoin'd
us to 't' (V, vi, 283–6). Even the child shares in the general corruption of humanity, in a world in which truth seems impossible,
where good and evil cannot be distinguished, and where the
only moral law appears to be a *nemesis* punishing sin with new sin
in a never ending cycle. Vittoria represents this disorder with its
constant confusion of opposites; she is the beauty which destroys:

> Your beauty! O, ten thousand curses on't.
> How long have I beheld the devil in crystal?
> Thou hast led me, like an heathen sacrifice,
> With music, and with fatal yokes of flowers
> To my eternal ruin.
>
> (IV, ii, 87–91)

So speaks Bracciano, reflecting the plight of man who cannot
distinguish appearance from reality, who is destroyed by evil in
his vain pursuit of what seems to be good and bears the outward
signs of beauty – music, yokes of flowers.

Bracciano's fate reminds the audience that in this world of
uncertainty and false appearance human aspirations are fruitless
and empty. Man's strivings can earn him only frustration, and
deeds come always to recoil upon the doer. The action of the play,
like that of *The Revenger's Tragedy*, is a structure of linked ironies.
While Camillo uses Flamineo, as he thinks, to win his duchess
back to him, Flamineo is, in fact, wooing her for Bracciano. The
symbol of the silkworm is used to express the human condition:
'Ha ha ha, thou entanglest thyself in thine own work like a silkworm' (I, ii, 196–7). All man's efforts lead to his own destruction,
and even pleasure is its own extinction; 'But all delight doth itself
soon'st devour' (I, ii, 204).

Francesco, lamenting the fate of his sister, cries out:

> would I had given
> Both her white hands to death, bound and lock'd fast
> In her last winding-sheet, when I gave thee
> But one.
>
> (II, i, 64–67)

The action will reveal that in giving her hand to Bracciano he has, in fact, given her to death. All greatness is a vain illusion in the world of *The White Devil*: 'Glories, like glow-worms, afar off shine bright, / But look'd to near, have neither heat nor light' (V, i, 41–42). Religion is a mask for evil. The elaborate election of the pope is followed by a linking of opposites: 'You have ta'en the sacrament to prosecute / Th' intended murder!' (IV, iii, 72–73) Even the act of devotion becomes the source of hatred and murder. The doctor knows how to 'poison a kiss' (II, i, 301), and Isabella dies kissing the poisoned portrait of her husband in a nightly ritual of love, just as Camillo has his neck broken in an act of friendly sport and fellowship. Bracciano is strangled with a 'true-love knot' (V, iii, 174), and his murderers are disguised as holy friars, supposedly working the salvation of his soul, while they remind him that he will 'die like a poor rogue . . . And stink like a dead fly-blown dog . . . And be forgotten before thy funeral sermon' (V, iii, 165–7). When he has been strangled, his murderers leave with holy words upon their lips: 'for charity, / For Christian charity, avoid the chamber' (V, iii, 172–3). We do not know whether the dying Bracciano's 'Vittoria? Vittoria!' (V, iii, 167) is a cry of horror or of all-consuming love.

Vittoria has been as beautiful as she has been evil; the dramatist has maintained towards her a moral ambivalence, and when she dies with courage and defiance, preserving her 'integrity of life' to the very end, we share imaginatively in a sense of heroism, of pride in the human condition, be it what it may. This sense of the heroic partially counteracts the feeling of despair created by the vision of an uncertain and chaotic world which we have beheld; it generates a pride in life itself. Delio, speaking for the author, offers a key to both plays in the final words of *The Duchess of Malfi*:

> Integrity of life is fame's best friend,
> Which nobly, beyond death, shall crown the end.
>
> (V, v, 145–6)

Vittoria's 'integrity of life' is the source of pride, and this pride growing out of evil is a reflection of the paradox in the play's title, that there may be good implicit in the darkest evil. This suggestion

Webster is to develop further in *The Duchess of Malfi*, that while
we exalt the fact of life itself we escape the chaos of a disordered
world. In *The White Devil* we see an evil woman attaining some
victory by her 'integrity of life', but we do not see the social
consequences which such integrity may have, its power to afford
a basis for morality. In his next play Webster goes on to show the
power of a pride in life to destroy some of the world's evils and
thus to justify the fact of human existence in a world seemingly
without other value. By this celebration of 'integrity of life',
Webster is not glorifying the ability of man to persevere in evil
as well as good, as some have supposed. He is celebrating a heroic
pride in the human condition which can win some victory even
to an evil Vittoria, but which when embodied in a virtuous
Duchess of Malfi may have power to effect a regeneration of the
social order.

Vittoria in her defiance stands for life, as her brother, Flamineo,
stands for death. 'You are, I take it, the grave maker' (V, iv, 80),
his mother says to him. His role is to deliver death directly to
others as he does to Camillo and Marcello, to instigate action
which will lead to death as he does for Bracciano, and to show the
others how to die when his own turn comes. For him death is
the only certainty in a world full of deception and uncertainty, the
only truth of which mankind is capable:

> Prosperity doth bewitch men seeming clear,
> But seas do laugh, show white, when rocks are near.
> We cease to grieve, cease to be Fortune's slaves,
> Nay, cease to die by dying.
>
> (V, vi, 250-3)

Unlike Bracciano, who strives for the goodness he sees in the love
of Vittoria and is led instead into desecration and death, Flamineo
accepts the world as a place of horror where felicity is never more
than sorrow in disguise, and he welcomes death as the final
certainty which ends man's slavery to such a world. Too many
commentators have equated Flamineo's view of the world with
Webster's tragic vision, but Flamineo stands only for the negation
from which Webster seeks to escape. Flamineo represents the
death force which Webster will oppose with a force of life,
sketched faintly in Vittoria and more surely in the Duchess of

Malfi. In the contrast between Vittoria and Flamineo, two figures of evil, Webster foreshadows what he is more fully to develop in the later play where the Duchess will oppose the principle of life to the death world represented by her brothers, with the imagery of their speeches underlining these symbolic functions, and with Bosola moving from the one side to the other, as Flamineo now is incapable of moving.

Flamineo is a Bosola incapable of growth. In a world in which he sees morality as impossible he seeks to prosper by a deliberate cultivation of the immoral. Like Shakespeare's Iago and Edmund he stands for the negation of order and harmony in the universe, for man without links either to God or his fellow men:

> I do not look
> Who went before, nor who shall follow me;
> No, at myself I will begin and end.
>
> (V, vi, 256–8)

He assumes the traditional role of the malcontent, exposing the evils of the world while he offers them as justification for his own 'Machiavellian policy'. Like Bosola, he comes upon the stage as one who has suffered through the world's evil, who has never prospered, but who now seeks to better his position by accepting the values of a universe without direction or moral law. He will live by 'policy', denying all human ties as he rejects his own mother and vaunts his immorality before her:

> Pray what means have you
> To keep me from the galleys, or the gallows?
> My father prov'd himself a gentleman,
> Sold all's land, and like a fortunate fellow,
> Died ere the money was spent. You brought me up
> At Padua I confess, where I protest
> For want of means, – the university judge me, –
> I have been fain to heel my tutor's stockings
> At least seven years: conspiring with a beard
> Made me a graduate, – then to this duke's service:
> I visited the court, whence I return'd
> More courteous, more lecherous by far,
> But not a suit the richer,—and shall I
> Having a path so open and so free
> To my preferment, still retain your milk

> In my pale forehead? no this face of mine
> I'll arm and fortify with lusty wine
> 'Gainst shame and blushing.
>
> (I, ii, 315–32)

The 'Machiavel' by Webster's day had become a conventional stage figure, a symbol for opposition to the moral order which cloaked itself in a mask of virtue. It stood for dissimulation. This is the code by which Flamineo lives, but it leads him to the same death which awaits his virtuous brother, Marcello.

There is no heroic quality in Flamineo's world. His speeches are full of cynicism, dwelling always on the base and sordid in human life; it is fitting that he be a pander. In his evil there is no 'integrity of life', for the 'Machiavel' to attain his ends must practise policy, seem to be what he is not, striking always under the guise of friendship, as when he betrays Camillo and his own sister. He is a mirror of the very indirection and confusion of the world he excoriates and which at last destroys him, but he never deceives himself. He accepts the world as he sees it, and we feel that could he have seen it otherwise, he might have lived otherwise. He is even made to feel remorse:

> I have liv'd
> Riotously ill, like some that live in court;
> And sometimes, when my face was full of smiles,
> Have felt the maze of conscience in my breast.
>
> (V, iv, 118–21)

His acceptance of death, paralleling the brave defiance of his sister, lends some note of grandeur to his end also, and the audience regrets the human waste for which he stands. In the later play Webster is to exhibit in Bosola the kind of redemption which was always possible in Flamineo, but which he could not achieve. Bosola enters *The Duchess of Malfi* proclaiming the same values as Flamineo, but before his death he learns from the Duchess what Flamineo never learns, that life itself can afford a basis for morality in a chaotic world.

III

In *The Duchess of Malfi* Webster returns to the 'mist' which is the world of *The White Devil*, but there is an immediate difference, for

the later play opens with Antonio's description of the emergence
of order and justice in France, and this conditions what follows,
for the audience has seen at the beginning the possibility of a
moral order, and nothing in the play can convince it of its impossibility. The two plays are linked by common motifs. Bosola
too calls the world 'a mist' (V, v, 118). Vittoria in *The White Devil*
dies lamenting the corruption of the court: 'O happy they that
never saw the court' (V, vi, 261), and dying Antonio at the
end of *The Duchess of Malfi* prays 'And let my son fly the courts
of princes' (V, iv, 84). The difference is that Vittoria could not
escape the evils of the world, whereas the son of Antonio will
have learned how to do so.

The moral statement of *The Duchess of Malfi* is not implicit in
the stock apothegms of such virtuous characters as Delio and
Pescara which, as has been observed, sometimes bear but slight
relation to the action and read – though, by no means, always –
like later additions.[1] It is implicit in the total imaginative impression of the play, for *The Duchess* is a unified work, with mood,
action, characterization and poetry all carefully shaped together
as an assertion of the inherent dignity of man. As part of this total
thematic statement the final act is of crucial importance, for its
function is to exhibit the effect upon the debased world of the
human spirit's triumph in spite of the body's destruction. The
particular effect of this tragedy is in its power to generate a tension
between our terror of a corrupt, disordered and chaotic universe
and our pride in the nobility of the human spirit which enables
man to survive and triumph in spite of such a world. In this
tension is Webster's moral vision, for the dignity of the human
spirit separates man from the baseness of the world, and the need
to preserve this dignity affords the true basis of morality. 'The
ultimate tragedy of Webster's world,' writes Travis Bogard
(p. 147), 'is not the death of any individual but the presence of evil
and decay which drags all mankind to death . . . the tragic story
is the story of a few who find courage to defy such revelation.
In their defiance there is a glory for mankind, and in their struggle
and assertion lies the brilliance of Websterian tragedy.' But this

[1] See Ian Jack, *Scrutiny*, XVI (1949), 38–43; M. E. Prior, *The Language of Tragedy*, pp. 32–33.

very sense of glory postulates a value which the evils of the world cannot destroy and which makes man superior to his world. It provides a frame of reference in which the relation of man to the forces of evil becomes apparent, and it leads not to a sense of despair but to one of tragic reconciliation.

When Webster's characters are considered in terms of psychological verisimilitude, glaring inconsistencies emerge. The venom of Ferdinand is poorly motivated. We rightly wonder why the brave soldier, Antonio, does not kill Ferdinand when he has ample opportunity in his wife's closet; or why Bosola should strangle the Duchess when he feels his greatest identity with her, and why he should later suffer remorse and reverse his allegiances. It is difficult to see why the cunning and self-assured Cardinal should continue to trust Bosola after the death of Julia has been revealed. None of this is explainable in terms of psychology or logical probability. The feeling of realism which Webster creates in spite of such improbabilities is the product of poetic illusion. His characters live in a world of imaginative symbol,[1] and they are shaped by the specific functions they are designed to perform as parts of the total dramatic unity.

The most important unifying element in *The Duchess of Malfi* is Bosola, a character whom critics have found particularly difficult to explain in terms of human psychology. The different roles he assumes as the play progresses may be reconciled to one another only in terms of the play's total thematic design. In the traditional pose of the malcontent he recapitulates the function of Flamineo in *The White Devil*, for he illuminates the evils of the world which will destroy the Duchess. As the instrument of the Arragonian brothers he shows this evil made explicit in action. In the death scene of the Duchess he serves a new and more complex function, for here he plays several roles, each designed to further the symbolism of the total scene. Primarily he is used to help the Duchess overcome her womanly fears and to arouse the spirit of greatness in her; he stands here for the nobility of the human spirit which he had opposed in his role as malcontent. Bosola must resolve the question posed by Cariola at the end of the first act: 'Whether the

---

[1] See F. P. Wilson, *Elizabethan and Jacobean* (Oxford, 1945), pp. 104–6; Edwards, pp. 157–8; Cecil, pp. 40–41.

spirit of greatness or of woman / Reign most in her, I know not'
(I, i, 576–7). 'Come, you must live' (IV, i, 81), says Bosola when
the Duchess is almost overcome with the horror of life and looks
to death for escape. When she has cursed the stars, vainly defying
an impersonal nature, rather than asserting her own integrity of
spirit, Bosola points out her folly: 'Look you, the stars shine still'
(IV, i, 120). 'In this climax,' writes Lucas (p. 187), 'Bosola's
cynicism rises to the sublime, as in four monosyllables he expresses the insignificance of human agony before the impassive
universe.' That the lines affirm the impassivity of the universe
and the insignificance of human suffering is, of course, true, but
to call them cynical is to ignore Bosola's role in the Duchess's
spiritual triumph and the traditional poetic associations of shining
stars. Man's awareness of the insignificance of his pain may help
him to rise above it. That 'the stars shine still' is a crucial statement of the play, for it is an assertion of the permanence and
indestructibility of nature. While the stars shine there is certainty,
for we cannot doubt the reality of the universe and of an illu-
minating beauty which persists in spite of all. The stars are a
symbol of hope which defeats the feeling of despair which the
horrors of the play may generate. Through the office of Bosola
the Duchess is able to assert the dignity of human life and meet
her death with the readiness and courage which are her triumph.[1]
To know the insignificance of human pain and the certainty of an
unextinguishable heavenly light is a means of escape from the
horrors of the world.

To view the death scene of the Duchess in a naturalistic perspective is to render it almost ludicrous. The ghastly horrors of

[1] See the fine discussion of Bosola's role in Bogard, pp. 67 ff. This very perceptive
study suffers from an over-emphasis upon the satiric in Webster which tends to
negate the value of the plays as tragedy. Webster, says Bogard (p. 5), 'made the
satiric voice coequal with the tragic, and in doing so brought together and steadily
controlled two all-but-incompatible attitudes towards human experience.' There is
an inherent contradiction in Bogard's thesis, for the two aspects he sees in Webster's
tragic vision are indeed incompatible. If Webster as a social satirist 'hoped his work
would arouse men to a concern for their world' (pp. 118–19), he could not well have
written the tragedies of negation and despair which Bogard finds. We cannot at the
same time have despair and a hope for social improvement. The satiric in Webster
is emphasized also by Rupert Brooke, *John Webster and Elizabethan Drama* (New
York, 1916), still valuable for some brilliant flashes of insight, and in Henry W.
Wells, *Elizabethan and Jacobean Playwrights* (New York, 1939), p. 46.

her torture are a symbolic portrait of the pain of the whole human condition, emphasizing as Flamineo had in *The White Devil* (V, vi, 252–3), that the process of living is itself a preparation for death. Before his sister in her final hours Ferdinand parades the ordinary condition of debased humanity: courtesans, bawds, ruffians and madmen. The various forms of madness represent the ordinary occupations of life:

> There's a mad lawyer and a secular priest,
> A doctor that hath forfeited his wits
> By jealousy: an astrologian,
> That in his works, said such a day o'th' month
> Should be the day of doom; and failing of 't
> Ran mad: an English tailor, crazed i'th' brain
> With the study of new fashions: a gentleman usher
> Quite beside himself with care to keep in mind
> The number of his lady's salutations,
> Or 'how do you', she employed him in each morning:
> A farmer too, an excellent knave in grain,
> Mad 'cause he was hindered transportation,
> And let one broker that's mad loose to these,
> You'ld think the devil were among them.
>
> (IV, ii, 49–62)

Doctor, lawyer, tailor, farmer and broker; these represent the ordinary affairs of the world, joined in a universal pageant of madness. This mad world is the world of Cariola, who will lie and beg, even plead pregnancy to spare her life; it is the world above which Bosola will help the Duchess to rise: 'When you send me next, / The business shall be comfort' (IV, i, 163–4).

In this symbolic portrait of a mad world decaying into death, Bosola, like Vindice in *The Revenger's Tragedy*, assumes several disguises, each indicating a different symbolic role. As the old maker of tombs he is a symbol of time and mutability, the destroyers of life, and he points to the impermanence and fragility of the human condition in words which recall those of Hamlet in the graveyard or Vindice with the skull of Gloriana:

> Thou art a box of worm seed, at best but a salvatory of green mummy. What's this flesh? a little curded milk, fantastical puff paste: our bodies are weaker than those paper prisons boys use to keep flies in; more contemptible, since ours is to preserve earthworms.

Didst thou ever see a lark in a cage? Such is the soul in the body:
this world is like her little turf of grass, and the heaven o'er our
heads, like her looking glass, only gives us a miserable knowledge of
the small compass of our prison.

(IV, ii, 123-31)

Bosola, like Hamlet and Vindice, is here speaking the commonplaces *de contemptu mundi*, a system of belief which, as we have seen,
emphasized the insignificance of the human body in order to make
clear the contrasting eternity of the soul. The lark in its cage
provides an image of striking power, stressing the ability of the
soul to soar towards heaven when the fragile cage of the body is
broken, just as the lark at daybreak flies straight towards the sun.
The heavens remind man of the smallness of his human body in
the light of eternity, just as the looking glass in the lark's cage
emphasizes the smallness of her prison. Bosola in this speech is
preparing the Duchess in conventional terms for a Christian stoic
acceptance of death as the liberation of the soul.[1]

Disguised as the bellman – whose traditional function was to
drive away evil spirits and to invite the faithful to pray for their
souls before death – Bosola stands for faith, penance, and the
hope of heaven which death affords. As the executioner with his
cord, he is the moment of death itself with its attendant pain.
When the Duchess awakens briefly before she dies, Bosola becomes a symbol of the comfort and mercy she will merit in
heaven. He tells her what she most longs to hear, that her loved
ones are still alive, and because of this the last word she utters is
'Mercy' (IV, ii, 381).

In the final act Bosola becomes the agent through which the
spirit of the Duchess is made to permeate the world. While Bosola
had accepted the values of Ferdinand and the Cardinal he had been
like them a symbol of death, the destroyer of life and beauty. The
final act is designed to show that the way of the Arragonian
brothers is that of madness and damnation, the complete descent
of man into beast symbolized by the lycanthropia of Ferdinand; it

[1] So also, John Donne in *The Second Anniversary*, while he celebrates the eternity
of the soul dwells upon the contrasting insignificance and physical loathsomeness of
the body, 'This curded milk, this poor unlittered whelpe/My body . . . a poore
Inne,/A Province pack'd up in two yards of skinne.'

shows also that the horrors for which they stand may be defeated
and rendered insignificant by a triumph of the indestructible
human spirit. This spirit forever separates man from the beast,
and it justifies human life in spite of the disorder which surrounds
it. Man need not fear to live so long as he can preserve his
'integrity of life' and die true to himself, with courage and acceptance; and while life itself has value we have a basis for morality.
This Bosola had learned from the death of the Duchess; now he
assumes her way and carries her values into the final act, becoming
an instrument of justice which affirms a moral order. His transformation may defy logical probability, but it is a symbol of
Webster's moral argument. When Bosola recognizes the value of
the Duchess's 'integrity of life', it is no longer possible for him to
live by the code which had linked him to the Arragonian brothers.
While good is possible, he must seek for values in life, and thus he
comes to stand for justice and the restoration of order. He now
can see the fate of Ferdinand not as an arbitrary reversal of fortune
in an uncertain and valueless world, but as a punishment for sin in
a world in which divine justice operates:

> Mercy upon me, what a fatal judgement
> Hath fallen upon this Ferdinand!
>
> (V, ii, 83-84)

This note of heavenly justice is in the nameless terror which comes
to haunt the Cardinal:

> When I look into the fishponds in my garden,
> Methinks I see a thing arm'd with a rake
> That seems to strike at me.
>
> (V, v, 5-7)

The guilty must be punished for their sins, and in the death of her
oppressors Bosola proclaims the victory of the Duchess:

> Revenge, for the Duchess of Malfi, murdered
> By th' Arragonian brethren; for Antonio,
> Slain by this hand; for lustful Julia,
> Poison'd by this man; and lastly, for myself
>
> (V, v, 102-5)

He executes vengeance even for the destruction of his own soul, and he willingly accepts the death and damnation which in the just moral order he now envisages are his due:

> It may be pain, but no harm to me to die
> In so good a quarrel. Oh this gloomy world,
> In what a shadow, or deep pit of darkness,
> Doth womanish and fearful mankind live!
> Let worthy minds ne'er stagger in distrust
> To suffer death or shame for what is just.
> Mine is another voyage.
>
> (V, v, 123–9)

He dies 'in so good a quarrel', and in his death there is an affirmation of justice. The new moral order is made visible in Antonio's young son who comes upon the stage as a symbol of rebirth. The theme of an emerging justice had been carried also in the death of Julia: 'I forgive you / This equal piece of justice you have done' (V, ii, 307–8). It had been prepared for also in Bosola's decision to aid the cause of Antonio:

> The weakest arm is strong enough, that strikes
> With the sword of justice. Still methinks the Duchess
> Haunts me.
>
> (V, ii, 379–81)

Bosola dies like the Duchess of Malfi, although he had lived most of his life in the service of those who would destroy her. Her death had been his regeneration:

> What would I do, were this to do again?
> I would not change my peace of conscience
> For all the wealth of Europe. She stirs; here's life;
> Return fair soul from darkness, and lead mine
> Out of this sensible hell.
>
> (IV, ii, 365–9)

Her 'fair soul', bright and unchanging like the shining stars, leads him out of the darkness of a world without value to an affirmation of the dignity of life for which she had stood and for which he now comes to stand. If the world is an abysmal chaos without guiding plan, in which good and evil must at last be made equal by the death which comes to all, man may still create his moral order, Webster in effect is saying, by upholding and preserving the dignity of human life. Death may destroy the body, but it cannot destroy the spirit. On one level, we may regard the play as the education of Bosola by the Duchess. He carries her values into the final act, where evil destroys itself and leaves behind only Delio, Pescara and Antonio's son, characters whose virtue is untainted. While he dwells on the blackness and pervasiveness of evil, Webster never allows us to forget the possibility of good; even in *The White Devil*, we have Isabella, Cornelia and Marcello whose virtue though sometimes hidden is always real.

The Duchess in her heroic opposition to her brothers is the symbol of life, as they are the symbols of death, and the play maintains a tension between the opposing forces of life and death, with the values of life at last triumphant. These symbolic functions of the Duchess and her brothers are carried in the poetic imagery of their lines.[1] Her only crime is 'that first good deed begun i'th' world, / After man's creation, the Sacrament of Marriage' (I, i, 437–8), and the generation of life to which it leads. Webster's source in William Painter's *Palace of Pleasure* had censured the Duchess for her lust, her neglect of the responsibilities of her station, and her avoidance of the rites of the church; of this censure there is no hint in Webster's play. Her courtship of Antonio is cast as a charming idyll with which we are meant to sympathize, and it is contrasted to the lustful Julia's attachment to the Cardinal. The Duchess asserts her ordinary human nature:

> This is flesh, and blood, Sir,
> 'Tis not the figure cut in alabaster
> Kneels at my husband's tomb. Awake, awake man;
> I do here put off all vain ceremony,
> And only do appear to you a young widow,
> That claims you for her husband.
>
> (I, i, 519–24)

She stands for the life of the flesh as opposed to the cold dead statue at the tomb, and her call is one of awakening. Her right to marry Antonio is an assertion of the basic claims of life, stripped of all ceremony. As she dies her thought is only of her children:

[1] The integral relation of imagery to action in Webster has been demonstrated ably by H. T. Price, *PMLA*, LXX (1955), 717–39. Cf. also Prior, *The Language of Tragedy*, pp. 120–35.

> I pray thee look thou giv'st my little boy
> Some syrup for his cold, and let the girl
> Say her prayers, ere she sleep.

(IV, ii, 207-9)

The inconsistency here, since she believes her children to be dead, has bothered critics, but Webster abandons logic for this striking emphasis upon his dying heroine as the creator and preserver of life. She has the power to 'raise one to a galliard / That lay in a dead palsy' (I, i, 200-1).

Her speeches are full of references to nature: birds, trees, the heavens, symbols of life and continuity. Bosola tells her, as we have seen, that the soul in the body is 'a lark in a cage', and she is identified with this soul by the image with which she describes herself:

> The robin redbreast and the nightingale,
> Never live long in cages.

(IV, ii, 15-16)

She compares herself and Antonio in their banishment to 'The birds that live i'th' field / On the wild benefit of nature' (III, v, 25-26), and she comes to see herself as such a bird fattened only for destruction: 'With such a pity men preserve alive / Pheasants and quails, when they are not fat enough / To be eaten' (III, v, 129-31). As she and Antonio celebrate their marriage they chorally relate their union to the life giving movement of the heavens:

> *Ant.* And may our sweet affections, like the spheres,
>   Be still in motion.
> *Duch.* Quickening, and make
>   The like soft music.
> *Ant.* That we may imitate the loving palms
>   (Best emblem of a peaceful marriage)
>   That never bore fruit divided.

(I, i, 551-7)

Webster uses a ritual technique to emphasize that the lovers stand for harmony, life and generation. Childbearing is a constant motif, and the speeches of Antonio and the Duchess are full of references to children:

I have seen children oft eat sweatmeats thus.

(I, i, 533)

. . . .

To see the little wanton ride a cock-horse
Upon a painted stick, or hear him chatter
Like a starling.

(I, i, 459–61)

The union of the bird and child images here makes clear their thematic function.

Ferdinand, the Cardinal, and Bosola while he serves them, stand in opposition as the destroyers of life, and the imagery of their speeches draws upon the destructive forces of nature. Ferdinand would

Root up her goodly forests, blast her meads,
And lay her general territory as waste,
As she hath done her honours.

(II, v, 27–29)

He will give her 'bastard' a handkerchief 'to make soft lint for his mother's wounds, when I have hewed her to pieces' (II, v, 39–42), and he will

boil their bastard to a cullis,
And giv't his lecherous father, to renew
The sin of his back.

(II, v, 92–94)

He stands for the desecration of parenthood, opposed to the generation of life.

The destructive, predatory animals are called up in the speeches of the Arragonian brothers. The Cardinal describes his mistress, Julia, as a hawk:

I have taken you off your melancholy perch,
Bore you upon my fist, and showed you game,
And let you fly at it.

(II, iv, 39–41)

They are bloodhounds, vipers, a tiger. The spring in the Cardinal's face is 'nothing but the engendering of toads' (I, i, 159–60). He and his brother are fed on by 'crows, pyes and catterpillers' (I, i, 52). The law to Ferdinand is 'a foul black cobweb to a spider'

(I, i, 181). He is 'a foul porpoise before / A storm' (III, iii, 64–65) . . . 'A very salamander lives in's eyes' (III, iii, 59). References to wolves continue to run through his lines until he emerges on the stage a wolf himself. Bosola refers to himself as a blackbird, a horse leech; he sees man as 'eaten up of lice, and worms' (II, i, 57); he is called a dormouse, an undermining mole, an impudent snake.

The Cardinal stands for the guile and hypocrisy which render religion but a shallow pretence. He carries on the traditional pose of the 'Machiavel', a symbol of evil wearing the mask of a seeming virtue. The function of his liaison with Julia is in part to emphasize this. If to display the death world of the Arragonian brothers were Webster's final purpose, as has so often been supposed, the tragedy would indeed be one of total despair, and as such it could not arouse those feelings of final acceptance and reconciliation upon which great tragedy depends. But this world is not the total picture. Into it comes the Duchess of Malfi who stands for the values of life, and Webster's final statement is that life may have nobility in spite of all. The Duchess, not her brothers, stands for ordinary humanity, love and the continuity of life through children. Her brothers stand only for death and decay – emphasized also by the disease imagery with which their speeches abound – and by Bosola's striking image:

> Your brother and yourself are worthy men!
> You have a pair of hearts and hollow graves,
> Rotten and rotting others.

> (III, ii, 344–6)

But the play asserts the final triumph of life over death. When all of the horrors of the world have been paraded before the Duchess and she faces the inevitable end in its most horrible form, she can still proclaim that 'I am Duchess of Malfi still' (IV, ii, 139). The body may be subject to death and decay, but in these words the Duchess affirms the permanence of the spirit which is the really vital part of man. The line in its simple syntax echoes Bosola's 'the stars shine still' (IV, i, 120), and equates the permanence of the human spirit with that of nature. This is Webster's answer to the pain of living and the fragility of the human condition.

Antonio is more central to the design of the play than usually
has been recognized. Although deeply involved in the action, he
is also a kind of choral commentator on it, for the audience is
invited to view the play through his eyes. He stands between the
death-world of the Arragonian brothers and the world of life
represented by the Duchess. He chooses life in spite of pain and
suffering, and like all who live he must suffer and die, his death
coming by a cruel accident of fate, as death so often does. But his
choice of the values of life enables him to accept death calmly and
to conquer the lust for revenge which might have accompanied
his injuries were he like Ferdinand. In spite of his suffering he
seeks at last for reconciliation. This is the first note sounded at
the opening of the final act:

> What think you of my hope of reconcilement
> To the Arragonian brethren?
>
> (V, i, 1–2)

There was no break between acts on the Jacobean stage, and the
word 'reconcilement', following hard upon the remorse of Bosola
which the audience has just beheld at the end of Act IV, would
give meaning to that remorse and show how it will dramatically
express itself. The initial note of 'reconcilement' conditions all
which is to follow in the final act. Antonio will go to the Cardinal's
chamber by the same means Ferdinand had used to enter that of
the Duchess, the parallel here being very deliberate, but he will go
to work good rather than evil:

> I have got
> Private access to his chamber, and intend
> To visit him about the mid of night,
> As once his brother did our noble Duchess.
> It may be that the sudden apprehension
> Of danger (for I'll go in mine own shape)
> When he shall see it fraught with love and duty,
> May draw the poison out of him, and work
> A friendly reconcilement.
>
> (V, i, 71–79)

This speech is crucial to an understanding of the play, for Antonio
is postulating a system of values – love, duty and reconciliation –

which in the world of Flamineo or the Arragonian brothers could not be possible.

It is the spirit of the Duchess which animates Antonio in the final act, just as it does Bosola, the one coming to stand for reconciliation and the other for justice. As Antonio dies he hears the names of his wife and children, and 'their very names / Kindle a little life in me' (V, iv, 68–69). In the echo scene the voice of the Duchess seeks to preserve his life, but Antonio has learned also from his wife that death is the inevitable end, and he accepts it calmly and peacefully. 'We are merely the stars' tennis balls, struck and bandied / Which way please them' (V, iv, 63–64), says Bosola. Man's pain is the product of a fickle fortune, but man may escape the bondage of fortune, as Antonio proves by the nobility of his endurance:

> Though in our miseries Fortune have a part,
> Yet in our noble sufferings she hath none –
> Contempt of pain, that we may call our own.
>
> (V, iii, 70–72)

Life may be full of pain and man a mere pawn in the hands of a capricious fate – all this Antonio recognizes in his death speech:

> In all our quest of greatness . . .
> Like wanton boys whose pastime is their care,
> We follow after bubbles blown in th'air.
> Pleasure of life, what is't? only the good hours
> Of an ague; merely a preparative to rest,
> To endure vexation. I do not ask
> The process of my death.
>
> (V, vi, 75–81)

To pursue greatness is as futile as to pursue pleasure; there is no escaping the pain and uncertainty of life, but the important lesson which Antonio has learned from his wife is how to 'endure vexation' in preparation for his everlasting rest. Webster affirms in Antonio's death that human aspirations are nothing, that the only good in life is the ability to endure life itself, and that man can 'fly the courts of princes' and the abysmal evil for which they stand, as Antonio would have his son to do (V, iv, 84), only by the assertion of the human quality which separates him forever

from the beasts: his ability to accept the pain and frustration of life
and to die with courage and dignity. This is the final moral statement to which all of the parts of *The Duchess of Malfi* were carefully
designed to give poetic expression, a resolution of the paradox
implicit in *The White Devil*.

CHAPTER SIX

Thomas Middleton

I

Thomas Middleton's plays are remarkable for a naturalistic technique which is almost unique in his age. It
appears [in the almost journalistic realism of his
comedies of London life, and among his tragedies in a depth of
psychological penetration and insight such as we find only in
Shakespeare. So striking is the psychological truth of characters
like his De Flores and Beatrice-Joanna in *The Changeling*, that it has
tended to obscure other elements in Middleton's art, and critics
often have been inclined to dismiss him as a kind of journeyman
craftsman capable at best of some moments of intense psychological insight, whose plays reveal little consistent unity of theme
or point of view. This is the judgment of T. S. Eliot,[1] and it has
been repeated, in effect, by the most recent editor of *The Changeling*,
who holds that 'the dramatist's interest, in other words, is psychological rather than philosophical'.[2] The masterful arguments by
William Empson and M. C. Bradbrook[3] for a close thematic
relation between main plot and sub-plot of *The Changeling* seem
to have had slight effect, for more recent critics of the play[4] still
dismiss the mad-house scenes of the sub-plot as William Rowley's

---

[1] *Selected Essays*, pp. 161–70. Ornstein, *The Moral Vision of Jacobean Tragedy*, sees
Middleton also as 'interested only in crucial moments of psychological and moral
tension' (p. 181).

[2] *The Changeling*, ed. N. W. Bawcutt (London, 1958), p. xlvii. See also G. R.
Hibbard, 'The Tragedies of Thomas Middleton and the Decadence of the Drama,'
University of Nottingham Renaissance and Modern Studies, I (1957), 35–64.

[3] William Empson, *Some Versions of Pastoral* (London, 1935), pp. 48–52; M. C.
Bradbrook, *Themes and Conventions of Elizabethan Tragedy*, pp. 213–24.

[4] Samuel Schoenbaum, *Middleton's Tragedies, A Critical Study* (New York), 1955),
pp. 132–49; R. H. Barker, *Thomas Middleton* (New York, 1958), pp. 121–31.
Ornstein, *The Moral Vision*, p. 180, sees the sub-plot as burlesquing the 'Petrarchan
conceits' of the main plot, but denies that 'plot and subplot form an organic unity
or that the subplot makes a significant enough contribution to the meaning of the
play to justify its repeated interruption of the main plot'.

heavy-handed intrusion of irrelevant farce into what might otherwise have been a greater play by Middleton, and the total product is judged an artistic failure.

I would suggest, on the contrary, that the realistic technique, not only of *The Changeling*, but of *Women Beware Women* as well, is merely the instrument by which Middleton effects a larger thematic design, and that in both plays the main plot and sub-plot are united by a common theme. Middleton is concerned not so much with the complexities of human character as with the nature of evil in the world, and each of his tragedies in its own way provides the emotional equivalent of a statement about man's relation to this evil. In this sense the tragedies of Thomas Middleton, like the others we have considered, are profoundly moral works. They embrace a more comprehensive view of human life than ever could be encompassed in the psychological study of any individual, no matter how intense or revealing.

The canon of Middleton's plays is obscure and confused, but with our present knowledge we can point to his achievement as a writer of tragedy in three plays, *Hengist, King of Kent*, *The Changeling*, and *Women Beware Women*. Of these, two are independent works, and *The Changeling* was written in a collaboration with William Rowley so close that the comic sub-plot, which seems to have been Rowley's principal contribution, was subsumed into the thematic unity of the whole. That Middleton's genius was the guiding spirit of the work there can be little doubt, and some light is thrown upon Middleton's achievement in tragedy when we consider *The Changeling*, which I would take to be the earlier play,[1] as Middleton's experiment with a dramatic technique and a moral theme which he was to extend and develop in *Women Beware Women*. I would suggest that the relation of these plays to one another is similar to that of *The White Devil* to *The Duchess of*

---

[1] Most commentators would date *The Changeling* in 1622. Since there is no reference of any sort to *Women Beware Women* before its entry in the Stationers Register in 1653, any suggestion must be conjectural, but stylistically it appears to be the later of the two works. R. C. Bald, 'The Chronology of Middleton's Plays,' *MLR*, XXXII (1937), 33–43, admits this, but nevertheless argues for a date in 1621 for reasons which G. E. Bentley has shown to be without merit. I would agree with Bentley that *Women Beware Women* is the later play, written some time shortly before Middleton's death in 1627. See *The Jacobean and Caroline Stage*, III, 906–7.

Malfi, and that the essence of Middleton's contribution to the tragedy of his age, like Webster's, is implicit in his two greatest plays.[1]

Middleton is Christian in his point of view, but we must recognize that his Christianity is of a distinct kind; it is neither that of Heywood nor of Tourneur. Heaven and hell are always present in Middleton's cosmos; the limits of good and evil are clear and well defined, and the sinner must inevitably suffer divine retribution. At the end of *The Changeling* there is a vindication of divine justice with the emergence of a new moral order; evil has been purged from society and new life is ready to begin. That we do not find such tragic reconciliation at the end of *Women Beware Women* may be the mark of an increasing pessimism combined with a broadening social range which causes the dramatist at last to see all of human society as corrupt and destined for destruction, with no redeeming qualities in man to offer any hope for the future. We do not have in *Women Beware Women* any of Shakespeare's faith in the heroic capabilities of man or of Heywood's belief in the power of love and human goodness to destroy evil. There is no suggestion of a divine providence guiding the affairs of men, in spite of their own indirection, to a rebirth of good, and there is little of Tourneur's confidence in a true felicity to be attained in heaven. Middleton's attention is fixed steadily on hell.

Middleton's plays are conditioned by a Calvinistic bias which leaves little room for the redemption of sinners. In *The Changeling* we find it expressed in the irrevocable damnation of individuals; in *Women Beware Women* it is extended to embrace the damnation of all mankind. The movement from the one play to the other is a movement from the specific to the universal. There is hope for the truly virtuous at the end of *The Changeling*, but *Women Beware Women* leaves us only with a feeling of frustration and waste, with a sense of the sordid ruin man has made of the world in which we

---

[1] *Hengist, King of Kent*, written some time between 1616 and 1620, is a lesser work which suffers from its crude sensationalism, but in which the basic tragic themes of Middleton nevertheless are present: the confusion of appearance with reality, the acceptance of evil out of an inherent moral blindness which makes man incapable of distinguishing it truly from the good, and his total degeneration as his own damnation gradually is revealed to him.

too must live, and with a feeling that this ruin is the product of an initial human commitment to evil which it is beyond the power of any man to alter. The play arouses no pride in the human condition, and we feel no sorrow for the destruction of any of the characters other than that conveyed in our sense of fellowship with them in damnation. These are not the emotions aroused by the tragedies of Shakespeare or any of the other writers of tragedy we have considered, but they are tragic emotions nevertheless, and they are products of a comprehensive vision of human life, terrible as that vision may be.

II

The Changeling is concerned not so much with the degeneration of Beatrice-Joanna, as is usually supposed, as with her coming, rather, to recognize and accept the evil which has always been a part of her, and which has been symbolized by the patient lurking figure of De Flores. There are no positive signs of virtue about the Beatrice-Joanna we first meet, only a wild, irrational horror of De Flores and his ugly dog face. She stands for an evil hidden from the world as it is hidden from herself. Her initial revulsion from De Flores seems in excess of any logical justification, but it is meaningful as the poetic symbol of her unwillingness to face the horror of what she really is. Beatrice-Joanna is damned from the first, and her slow acceptance of her own damnation is portrayed with an amazing psychological truth. The action of the main plot is a realistic portrayal of the stripping away of her mask of virtue, 'a visor / o'er that cunning face' (V, ii, 46–47). This stripping is effected by a series of moral choices, in each of which Beatrice-Joanna thinks that she is choosing by judgment, but in which she is directed instead by a blind will over which she has no control and which is in direct opposition to judgment.

Her self-deception is made clear at the beginning of the play:

> Our eyes are sentinels unto our judgments,
> And should give certain judgment what they see;
> But they are rash sometimes, and tell us wonders
> Of common things, which when our judgments find,
> They can then check the eyes, and call them blind.
>
> (I, i, 71–76)

The power of the eye to beguile judgment is a repeated motif. Beatrice-Joanna thinks always that her acts are guided by reason and wisdom. While she awaits the news of the murder she has commissioned, for instance, she prides herself upon her rational powers:

> So wisdom by degrees works out her freedom;
> And if that eye be darkened that offends me
> (I wait but that eclipse), this gentleman
> Shall soon shine glorious in my father's liking,
> Through the refulgent virtue of my love.
>
> (III, iv, 13–17)

Her wisdom is merely the delusion that love can grow out of murder, and we know that she has already forfeited her claim to the virtue on whose power she so prides herself. The polar opposites in the poetic imagery – sunlight growing out of eclipse – point to the contradiction inherent in her position and brand her speech as the grossest self-deception and moral equivocation. It is not her judgment but her will which, in fact, governs all her conduct.

Miss Bradbrook has pointed to the constant repetition in the play of 'judgment' and 'will'. When De Flores proclaims that 'Though I get nothing else, I'll have my will' (I, i, 240), he is indicating that his pursuit of Beatrice-Joanna springs from the kind of passion which destroys judgment. The eclipse of judgment is in the kind of specious moral equivocation with which Beatrice-Joanna counters De Flores's demand:

> Why, 'tis impossible thou canst be so wicked,
> Or shelter such a cunning cruelty,
> To make his death the murderer of my honour!
> Thy language is so bold and vicious,
> I cannot see which way I can forgive it
> With any modesty.
>
> (III, iv, 120–5)

The moral blindness which cannot perceive that in the act of murder is the denial of honour and modesty is the sign of the heroine's commitment to evil. From this blindness she must make two movements: she must come first to see her own evil, and she must come then willingly to embrace it. De Flores first strips her blindness from her:

> Push, you forget yourself!
> A Woman dipped in blood and talk of modesty?
>
> (III, iv, 125–6)

When she has recognized her own damnation Beatrice-Joanna can only grow closer and closer to De Flores who is the symbol of this damnation, until they are as surely united as Shakespeare's Othello is to Iago. Their union is expressed by Middleton in terms of their sexual relation and in the increasing intimacy of their speeches until Beatrice, recognizing both the falseness of her own claim to honour and her closeness to De Flores, can say:

> I am forced to love thee now,
> 'Cause thou provid'st so carefully for my honour.
>
> (V, i, 47–48)

His physical ugliness at last becomes inconsequential, for the ugliness of her own soul has been revealed:

> How heartily he serves me! His face loathes one,
> But look upon his care, who would not love him?
> The east is not more beauteous than his service.
>
> (V, i, 70–72)

De Flores, with his 'Let me go to her, sir' (V, iii, 110), can assert a right which is greater than her husband's, and which the husband recognizes:

> Nay, you shall to her.
> Peace, crying crocodile, your sounds are heard!
> Take your prey to you, get you in to her, sir.
> I'll be your pander now; rehearse again
> Your scene of lust, that you may be perfect
> When you shall come to act it to the black audience
> Where howls and gnashings shall be music to you.
> Clip your adult'ress freely, 'tis the pilot
> Will guide you to the Mare Mortuum,
> Where you shall sink to fathoms bottomless.
>
> (V, iii, 111–20)

In this speech is a summation of Beatrice-Joanna's relation to De Flores. Her tears are the false tears of the crocodile; she has from the first been the destined prey of the waiting De Flores, and now joined inseparably they will go to hell where the sounds of the damned will provide fit accompaniment for their lust. The progression of Beatrice-Joanna from a choice of evil through a moral blindness which is the product of her own damnation, to a full awareness of evil, and at last to a willing embrace of damnation, is the typical Middleton progression. It involves not a process of transformation, but rather the stripping away of false pretence to reveal an inner corruption which has always existed. The characters upon whom Middleton concentrates his tragic focus – Beatrice-Joanna, De Flores, Leantio, Bianca – never have any real choice. They are damned to begin with, and they need only learn that this is so.

There is a significant difference between *The Changeling* and *Women Beware Women* in this respect. In the earlier play Middleton shows us the reality of damnation in the inescapable fate of Beatrice-Joanna, but he shows us also the grace of God which can preserve Isabella. On a lesser scale she is faced with a like temptation and shown a like vision of evil, but she is able to make a proper moral choice and thus escape damnation. The world of *The Changeling* is full of evil, but the sub-plot reveals also the possibility of good, and this is one reason that Isabella and her lovers are so essential to the total play. In *Women Beware Women* we are never shown the possibility of good, only an invidious evil corrupting every level of society through the same kind of moral equivocation which is the mark of Beatrice-Joanna's damnation. The dating of the two plays, of course, is uncertain, but if no great time elapsed between them, we may perhaps account for the more optimistic moral vision of *The Changeling* by the share of William Rowley in that play. That he was principally responsible for the sub-plot may lend some support to this supposition.

The changeling of the title may refer, as has been suggested often, both to Antonio and Beatrice-Joanna; if so the reference to the heroine would be an ironic one, for what seems to be her transformation from virtue the play reveals to have been, in reality, no change at all. The term has been applied also to Diaphanta and by Empson to De Flores as well. Properly it fits only Antonio, the disguised fool, for which changeling was a

common term; the changes in character are only seeming ones.
The dominant motif of the play is the working out of a kind of
inexorable fate which makes impossible any real change. The
feeling of ominous foreboding is established in the opening speech:

> 'Twas in the temple where I first beheld her,
> And now again the same; what omen yet
> Follows of that?
>
> (I, i, 1–3)

Alsemero has met Beatrice-Joanna in a church, the place of holiness where divine purpose is expressed, and now he is meeting
her there again. Fate seems to have brought them together, and he
looks for meaning in their encounter. His faith in the holiness of
his own purpose, marriage, leads him to accept his destiny, whatever it may be:

> Why should my hopes or fate be timorous?
> The place is holy, so is my intent.
>
> (I, i, 4–5)

His friend, Jasperino, is amazed by the strangeness of his conduct,
but Alsemero cannot sail with the tide as he had planned; his
fate decrees otherwise:

> Even now I observ'd
> The temple vane to turn full in my face.
> I know 'tis against me.
>
> (I, i, 19–21)

He seems to be directed by 'some hidden malady / Within me, that
I understand not' (I, i, 24–25).

The power of a controlling destiny is made clear by the questions Beatrice-Joanna and Alsemero ask of the audience. 'Did my
fate wait for this unhappy stroke / At my first sight of woman?'
(V, iii, 12–13), asks Alsemero when the horror of his marriage has
been revealed to him, and Beatrice-Joanna asks when she sees her
inevitable union with De Flores: 'Was my creation in the womb
so curs'd, / It must engender with a viper first?' (III, iv, 165–6),
recalling also the sin of Eve. Before her death she explains that
her damnation has been the working out of a terrible destiny:

> Beneath the stars, upon yon meteor
> Ever hung my fate, 'mongst things corruptible;

I ne'er could pluck it from him: my loathing
Was prophet to the rest, but ne'er believed;
Mine honour fell with him, and now my life.
                                    (V, iii, 154–8)

De Flores is the meteor, the traditional symbol in Elizabethan and
Jacobean cosmology of change and decay, opposed to the constancy and permanence of the stars. She is saying that her very
loathing of De Flores was a sign of her destined link to him which
she could not evade, that in it her damnation was implicit from
the first. She has known the horror of a terrible self-discovery.

Although all of the characters seek to act by judgment, they
are led by something within them which is stronger than human
judgment and which will have its way. They cannot know their
own motives or the motives of each other until fate is ready to
reveal them. Of this human impotence in the face of divine will,
Alsemero's virginity test is a dramatic symbol. It has been
censured by critics as ridiculous melodrama. I would suggest that
its very ludicrousness is a part of Middleton's design, to illustrate
the futility of any probing into what only time can reveal. With
all his skill and wisdom, the learned doctor cannot discern the
evil which is always before him.

The primary focus of the main plot is upon Beatrice-Joanna
and De Flores; the other characters serve to create the complex of
action in which the heroine must undergo her tragic role, and
they are used also to represent contrasting positions which man
may take in the face of evil. Diaphanta's role is parallel to that of
her mistress. She is a changeling in a double sense, as the sub-
stitute for her mistress in the marriage bed, and as one whose outward appearance of virtue, 'As good a soul as ever lady counte-
nanc'd' (V, i, 101), will be changed by the temptation of gold to
that of the whore which she really is and who will be destroyed
by De Flores as he destroys her mistress. The perverted judgment
of the heroine is paralleled by that of Alonzo de Piracquo who,
in spite of the warning of his brother, sees the evil of Beatrice-
Joanna as good and is destroyed by his inability to distinguish
appearance from reality. His brother, Tomazo, hangs over the
play as a figure of *nemesis*, but he is an ineffective one, not knowing
where to strike, no more capable than Alsemero of finding evil

where it lurks. He is spared at the end from the sin of murder only by time's revelation of the answer he seeks.

Tomazo stands for human confusion and frustration before the reality of an evil which he perceives but does not understand. He needs to strike at evil, and his inability to do so with certain knowledge embitters his existence while he casts about vainly for some answer:

> I cannot taste the benefits of life
> With the same relish I was wont to do.
> Man I grow weary of, and hold his fellowship
> A treacherous bloody friendship; and because
> I am ignorant in whom my wrath should settle,
> I must think all men villains, and the next
> I meet (who'er he be) the murderer
> Of my most worthy brother.
>
> (V, ii, 1–8)

He lives 'in the state of ignorance' in a world of false appearance where 'A brother may salute his brother's murderer / And wish good speed to th'villain in a greeting' (V, ii, 46–48), and he is incapable of escape from this condition.

That the wise Alsemero is deceived by Beatrice-Joanna's hidden evil illustrates also the general fallibility of human judgment and reinforces the fatalism of the play. He echoes the plight of all mankind in his final realization of the evil which has betrayed him:

> Oh cunning devils!
> How should blind men know you from fair fac'd saints?
>
> (V, iii, 108–9)

He is a learned doctor whose wisdom can reveal the secrets of nature, and he is a man of uncompromising virtue:

> Oh, were she the sole glory of the earth,
> Had eyes that could shoot fire into kings' breasts,
> And touch'd, she sleeps not here!
>
> (IV, ii, 105–7)

Even the virtue and wisdom of such a man, representing the ultimate in human power, cannot unmask an evil wearing the outward signs of good. Fate must work out its course. Alsemero is deceived, but he never deceives himself, and he is guilty of no moral equivocation. His remorseless pursuit of the truth leads to the final revelation of evil when fate is ready to reveal it, and Alsemero must remain alive at the end of the play to stand for the birth of a new moral order.

De Flores is the symbol of damnation. To him Beatrice-Joanna is pledged, and he waits patiently until by her own action he is given the chance to claim his due. He also is driven by a remorseless fate; he cannot choose but haunt his prey:

> Must I be enjoyn'd
> To follow still while she flies from me? Well,
> Fates do your worst.
>
> (I, i, 101–2)

> I know she hates me,
> Yet cannot choose but love her.
>
> (I, i, 235–6)

> I can as well be hang'd as refrain seeing her.
>
> (II, i, 28)

Her virginity stands for the shallow pretence of virtue which at first keeps her from him, and this virginity he must destroy:

> And were I not resolv'd in my belief
> That thy virginity were perfect in thee,
> I should but take my recompense with grudging,
> As if I had but half my hopes I agreed for.
>
> (III, iv, 116–19)

When the murder has been committed he can claim her soul with as much right as the devil claimed that of Marlowe's Faustus. She belongs to him entirely, his equal and his mate:

> Look but into your conscience, read me there,
> 'Tis a true book, you'll find me there your equal:
> Push, fly not to your birth, but settle you
> In what the act has made you, y'are no more now;
> You must forget your parentage to me:
> Y'are the deed's creature; by that name
> You lost your first condition, and I challenge you,

> As peace and innocency has turn'd you out,
> And made you one with me.
>
> (III, iv, 132–40)

The words are chilling in their realistic intensity, and they may
have larger symbolic overtones. There is the suggestion that
De Flores in claiming Beatrice-Joanna is the devil himself claiming fallen man. The lost 'first condition' may refer also to man's
state of innocence before the Fall, and to be 'the deed's creature'
may be to share in the original sin of mankind. That Beatrice-
Joanna's delivery to De Flores represents the final working out of
an inexorable destiny is reinforced by the horror of his cold reply
to her plea for mercy:

> Can you weep fate from its determined purpose?
> So soon may you weep me.
>
> (III, iv, 162–3)

From this moment forward Beatrice-Joanna is joined to De
Flores and they are, in fact, already in hell together. This is at
last made clear by De Flores:

> Yes; and the while I coupled with your mate
> At barley-brake; now we are left in hell.
>
> (V, iii, 162–3)

The game of barley-brake was played with a central area known
as hell. Through this area various couples ran together while the
couple in hell tried to catch them, those caught remaining to take
their turn in hell. It was a popular pastime of the age, and this
game is made to represent the action of the play. Beatrice-Joanna
and De Flores have been the couple in hell throughout. Others
have run through but managed to escape, and at the end of the
play only they remain. There is a terrible pessimism in the re-
joinder of Vermandero: 'We are all there, it circumscribes here'
(V, iii, 164). This is the motif to which Middleton will return in
Women Beware Women.

The barley-brake symbol is only one of several by which the
main plot and sub-plot are united. No sooner has Antonio cast
off his disguise and begun to court Isabella than a madman calls
out in the background, 'Catch there, catch the last couple in hell!'
(III, ii, 165.) Isabella and Antonio are playing also at barley-brake,

and to show their ability to escape hell is an important function of the sub-plot. It would be futile to argue that the scenes in the madhouse of Alibius add much to the artistry of the play. They are crude, farcical, generally in bad taste, and full of extraneous comic horseplay. They represent the kind of comic hackwork for which William Rowley is known. But to say that the sub-plot is crudely executed and in bad taste is not to say that it is unrelated to the central theme of the play. The sub-plot shows links with the main plot which are deliberate and unmistakeable. Miss Brad-brook has seen the relation as that of anti-masque to masque.

Isabella provides a counterpart for Beatrice-Joanna. Her marriage to Alibius may be compared to the engagement of Beatrice-Joanna to Alonzo de Piracquo, for it involves a like restraint. Isabella is tempted to break her bonds not once but twice, by Antonio and Franciscus, and it may be because Middleton wishes to emphasize the ability of Isabella to stand firm in spite of temptation that he provides her with two suitors rather than one. Lollio is witness to her courtship by Antonio, and he demands the same price for his silence as De Flores had demanded for Beatrice-Joanna's safe marriage to Alsemero. Isabella's reply is a direct reversal of Beatrice-Joanna's:

> Sirrah, no more! I see you have discovered
> This love's knight-errant, who hath made adventure
> For purchase of my love; be silent, mute,
> Mute as a statue, or his injunction
> For me enjoying, shall be to cut thy throat:
> I'll do it, though for no other purpose,
> And be sure he'll not refuse it.
>
> (III, iii, 237–44)

Lollio has been the tempter of Isabella, showing her the prospective lovers, willing to keep their assignations secret, demanding only her virtue as his fee: 'My share, that's all; I'll have my fool's part with you' (III, iii, 245). She destroys his power over her, as Beatrice-Joanna could not and would not destroy that of De Flores, by turning his own instrument against him. If she must surrender her virtue, her surrender will be the death of her tempter and not his gratification. We are shown the kind of triumph over evil of which Isabella because of her innocence is capable, but of which Beatrice-Joanna because of the evil already within her is not.

There may be in the sub-plot also the suggestion that while Antonio wears the disguise of the fool he too can escape evil, thus reinforcing the theme that it is not through human reason that man may escape evil, but only through a native innocence with which some few are endowed by the grace of God. Antonio woos Isabella only in his proper shape, never in disguise, and in this there is the suggestion that only when he casts off the role of the fool does he risk damnation. This is implicit in Isabella's rejection of his suit:

> Fie, out again! I had rather you kept
> Your other posture: you become not your tongue,
> When you speak from your clothes.

(III, iii, 170-2)

His 'other posture' is his fool's habit. The fool, as the special child of God, saved by a heavenly grace greater than the power of human reason, is a familiar motif in the world's literature. We may find some reflection of it in the Fool in *King Lear*.

The theme is not developed consistently or at length, but there may be also in the division of Alibius's house into fools and madmen a suggestion that the entire world is so divided and that these are the elect and the damned of Calvinist theology. The fools can escape damnation through divine grace; the madmen represent judgment vitiated by will, and they engage in moral equivocation which is the result of fallible human reason. Antonio's first temptation of Isabella is followed by the entrance of a chorus of madmen dressed as animals and birds. They emphasize, as Miss Bradbrook has pointed out, the bestiality of man, and they serve as ritualistic commentary upon the action of Antonio.

Similarly, when Isabella decides finally to test the love of Antonio, she appears to him disguised as a madwoman. The 'wild unshapen antic' (IV, iii, 125) who confronts him shows him that lust is madness. In Antonio's rejection of what he once had sought is the salvation of both, for Antonio has seen lust in its true form as misshapen madness, and Isabella has seen his illicit pursuit of her as judgment warped by will which has led only to a worship of outward appearance:

> No, I have no beauty now,
> Nor never had, but what was in my garments.
> You a quick-sighted lover? Come not near me!
> Keep your caparisons, y'are aptly clad;
> I came a feigner to return stark mad.
>
> (IV, iii, 131-5)

He is 'aptly clad' as a fool, and she rejects his illicit passion because he is a fool. His reason has been as defective as that of even the wise Alsemero, but he has been protected by his guise of folly. There is a double meaning in his final admission of the lesson he has learned:

> Yes, sir; I was chang'd too, from a little ass as I was, to a great fool as I am, and had like to ha' been chang'd to the gallows, but that you know my innocence always excuses me.
>
> (V, iii, 204-7)

By his 'innocence' he means not only his freedom from actual guilt, but the guise of folly which has preserved him.

The two plots are brought together in the final scene of the play. Vermandero here sees in his daughter's damnation a sign of his own defilement and of the general damnation of mankind, but Alsemero points to the rebirth of good in a mood of tragic reconciliation:

> justice hath so right
> The guilty hit, that innocence is quit
> By proclamation, and may joy again.
> Sir, you are sensible of what truth hath done;
> 'Tis the best comfort that your grief can find.
>
> (V, iii, 183-9)

This is Middleton's final affirmation of a justice and order in the universe from which man may draw some comfort in spite of the evil all around him. In the destruction of Beatrice-Joanna he has shown the terrible reality of damnation, but he has shown also that evil is self-destructive, and particularly in his sub-plot, he has affirmed the possibility of good.

III

Women Beware Women has been more harshly treated by critics than *The Changeling*. It has been dismissed usually as a play of some

powerful realistic scenes which falls to pieces at the end in the
crude sensationalism of its multiple murder scene. The characters have been condemned for their utter and unredeemed
depravity. I would suggest that the sordid realism of the characterization and the mass murders at the end are not artistic defects;
they are conditioned and made necessary by the particular moral
statement which the total play affirms. *Women Beware Women*
extends the damnation of Beatrice-Joanna on to a social range, so
that the play becomes the dramatic symbol of the damnation of all
mankind. Each of the moral choices in this play involves the same
kind of moral equivocation we have noted in the earlier play, a
self-deception leading to a choice of evil in the delusion that it is
good. Sub-plot and main plot again are closely related, all of the
elements of the play combining to shape an ethical statement.
Middleton shows his audience a dismal picture of a doomed mankind manifesting its own inherent damnation by a deification of
worldly success and false appearance.

The play's action is a neatly interwoven series of moral choices.
In the main plot these are made by Leantio, Bianca and the Duke,
and in the sub-plot by Isabella, Hippolito and the Ward, and with
a lesser emphasis, by Guardiano and Fabricio. Some of these
choices have been made before the action opens. Each of the main
characters pays homage to the outward signs of virtue, but each
is willing to sin so that these outward signs may be preserved;
one evil is embraced willingly so as to avoid the mere appearance
of another. The Ward and his man, with the appropriate name
Sordido, are used as comic commentary on this moral equivocation and self-deception. Livia and the Cardinal stand apart, she
in her complete and willing rejection of all moral values, and he
in his rejection of the worldly values by which the others live and
in his role as prophet of the retribution which inevitably must
follow. All of the others are moral equivocators, and moral
equivocation sets the dominant tone of the play. The final scene of
mass murder is necessary and proper. It is not to be explained in
terms of logical credibility, but rather as the dramatic symbol of
the inevitable collapse of a society which by a faulty choice of
values inherent in the very nature of humanity has devoted itself
to its own destruction. If it catered to a Jacobean taste for the

spectacular, it is also the necessary culmination to the moral argument of the play.

Middleton's technique is highly realistic, but there is also an important symbolic element in his dramatic art. A failure to recognize this has led some critics to attribute to Middleton's supposed illogic and his love of the spectacular elements which are perfectly meaningful as part of a ritual technique designed to emphasize an underlying theme. This element of ritual is reflected in the conscious patterning of the action which borrows much from the technique of masque and anti-masque. The seduction of Bianca, for instance, is paralleled by Livia's move in the game of chess which she and Leantio's mother play below, so that seduction and chess game together take on the qualities of a ritual dance.[1] At the banquet scene in the third act the Ward's grotesque dance with Isabella follows closely upon her dance with Hippolito; by burlesquing Hippolito's movements the Ward emphasizes the sordid pretence and self-deception of the lovers. This element of ritualistic parody reaches its height in the final banquet scene where the principal characters destroy one another in the elaborate ritual of a marriage masque, the grotesque incongruity of the masque emphasizing that of the actual marriage of Bianca to the Duke at which it is performed.

In *The Changeling* Middleton does not rely heavily upon his poetic imagery to carry the theme; there are the obvious associations of De Flores with poison, but little more. In this regard *Women Beware Women* shows a considerable advance in Middleton's artistry, for in the later play the poetic imagery is highly developed and systematized, and it is one of the principal devices by which the main plot and sub-plot are linked. By recurrent imagery Middleton underlines the common theme to which the various relationships of the play contribute. Each of the principal characters is highly realistic, but each also is a dramatic symbol of moral equivocation. Each comes to that awareness of his own corruption so well exemplified in Beatrice-Joanna. The characters of *Women Beware Women* are not lovable, but Middleton creates the feeling that, taken all together, they stand for humanity, and the total play, with each self-destructive character emphasizing

[1] Barker, *Thomas Middleton*, pp. 142–4, has perceived Middleton's ritual technique.

the parallel self-destruction of the others, becomes the tragedy of humanity at large.

The destructive values which Middleton most strongly castigates are those of worldly success and worldly pleasure, the very values which in the medieval philosophy *de contemptu mundi* gave strongest evidence of damnation. This concern is reflected in poetic imagery drawn from commercial exchange and from gluttonous feeding.[1] The function of the imagery is not merely to condition the mood, although it certainly does this, but chiefly to convey poetically a sense of the sordid shallowness of each of the play's moral choices in the very lines in which the particular choice is made. Imagery is further used to link these moral choices to one another and thus to keep always in the consciousness of the audience the interconnection among them which sustains the social range of the tragedy.

The two crucial episodes of moral commitment at the beginning of the third act, for instance, are linked to one another by imagery drawn from food and commerce: Isabella's acceptance of the Ward as a cover for her incestuous relation to Hippolito is linked by recurring motifs to Bianca's departure from Leantio to be the open concubine of the Duke.

Isabella is sold to the Ward by her father as he would sell a horse:

> Nay, you shall see, young heir, what you've for your money,
> Without fraud or imposture.
>
> (III, ii, 75–76)

The Ward emphasizes the sordidness of Fabricio's offer by comic parody as he considers his prospective marriage in the same terms, and his language is full of references to feasting:

> I have seen almost
> As tall as she sold in the fair for tenpence:
> See how she simpers it, as if marmalade
> Would not melt in her mouth! she might have the
>   kindness i' faith,
> To send me a gilded bull from her own trencher,

---

[1] The dominance of this type of imagery has been noted by Miss Bradbrook, *Themes and Conventions*, pp. 234–9, but it is much more highly 'systematized' than she has indicated and much more closely related to the total structure of the play.

A ram, a goat, or somewhat to be nibbling:
These women, when they come to sweet things once,
They forget all their friends, they grow so greedy,
Nay, oftentimes their husbands.

(III, ii, 69–77)

Middleton makes clear to his audience that Isabella has accepted the very values of her father and the Ward as, intent upon her lust for Hippolito, she allows herself to be examined like a horse for sale, accompanying her voluntary choice of evil with the same imagery drawn from food and commerce:

But that I have th' advantage of the fool,
As much as woman's heart can wish and joy at,
What an infernal torment 'twere to be
Thus bought and sold, turned and pry'd into,
When, alas,
The worst bit's too good for him! and the comfort is
Has but a cater's place on't and provides
All for another's table.

(III, iii, 33–40)

She sees herself as superior to the Ward, as unaware as Beatrice-Joanna that by her own act she is revealing herself to the audience as his equal in vice. She has never really been anything else.

Similarly in the main plot, Leantio's mother will 'trot into a bawd now / For some dry sucket, or a colt in march-pane' (III, i, 269-70). She has been charged with the protection of Bianca's virtue; her complete abandonment of her trust is rendered sordid and ludicrous by the imagery of the speech in which it is couched:

I'll first obey the Duke,
And taste of a good banquet; I'm of thy mind:
I'll step but up and fetch two handkerchiefs
To pocket up some sweetmeats, and o'ertake thee.

(III, i, 265–8)

The virtue she has been charged to protect has been as non-existent as her ability to protect it. Not only in these two crucial episodes, but throughout the play, the poetry is dominated by references to food, and the casting of the play's moral choices in the crass terms of commerce is reflected again and again. It appears in the very profession of Leantio, the factor.

In the opening scene of the play Leantio describes his stolen bride as 'the most unvalud'st purchase / That youth of man had ever knowledge of' (I, i, 12–13). She is his 'life's wealth' (III, ii, 207), his treasure, and even his enjoyment of her is expressed in commercial terms:

> 'Tis a bitterness
> To think upon to-morrow! that I must leave
> Her still to the sweet hopes of the week's end;
> That pleasure should be so restrain'd and curb'd
> After the course of a rich work-master,
> That never pays till Saturday night! marry
> It comes together in a round sum then,
> And does more good, you'll say.
>
> (I, i, 154–61)

He praises that love which is 'respective for increase' (I, iii, 47), and when Bianca has been discovered by the Duke, Leantio will lock up his treasure as a miser hoards his gold:

> At the end of the dark parlour there's a place
> So artifically contriv'd for a conveyance
> No search could ever find it . . .
> There will I lock my life's best treasure up.
>
> (III, i, 244–8)

The word 'conveyance' reminds the audience that Bianca has been stolen, and in its secondary meaning it has further connotations of commerce, the transfer of property. This commercial imagery is combined with that of feasting; wedlock to Leantio is 'like a banqueting house' (III, i, 90), and he sees his absence from Bianca's bed as 'a five days' fast' (III, i, 106).

Leantio in the first act does not represent the idealistic and devoted lover which critics have sometimes seen in him. The imagery drawn from feasting and commerce which infuses his speeches adds a note of the base and sordid to the quality of his devotion and supports the feeling that his degeneration is already implicit in the moral choice – the theft of a bride – which he has made before the opening of the action. He is not to be regarded as a loving, virtuous husband whose decline will be the theme of the play. He will merely come to learn the depths of his own evil and debasement, as it was learned by Beatrice-Joanna in *The Changeling*, as it is learned by Bianca and by every other of this play's major characters.

Leantio's very devotion to Bianca involves a kind of moral equivocation, for while he protests the purity of his love and his superiority to other men in virtue because of it, he admits the theft of Bianca from her parents and the consequent loss of dowry which will force them both to live in poverty:

> I find no wish in me bent sinfully
> To this man's sister, or to that man's wife;
> In love's name let 'em keep their honesties,
> And cleave to their own husbands – 'tis their duties:
> Now when I go to church I can pray handsomely,
> Nor come like gallants only to see faces,
> As if lust went to market still on Sundays.
> I must confess I'm guilty of one sin, mother,
> More than I brought into the world with me,
> But that I glory in; 'tis theft, but noble
> As ever greatness yet shot up withall.
>
> (I, i, 28–38)

But theft cannot be noble, and a virtue dependent upon such theft is vitiated at its very source; it is only a seeming virtue which hides an inner corruption. This very theft, with its resulting poverty for the lovers, will destroy them both.

Lust goes ever 'to market', and when Leantio sees Bianca's surrender to lust and his own reward of a captainship for his cuckoldry, his speech again fuses the imagery of commercial husbandry and gluttonous feasting:

> a fine bit
> To stay a cuckold's stomach: all preferment
> That springs from sin and lust it shoots up quickly,
> As gardeners' crops do in the rotten'st grounds;
> So is all means raised from base prostitution
> Even like a salad growing upon a dunghill.
> I'm like a thing that never was yet heard of,
> Half merry and half mad: much like a fellow
> That eats his meat with a good appetite,
> And wears a plague-sore that would fright a country;
> Or rather like the barren, harden'd ass

That feeds on thistles till he bleeds again;
And such is the condition of my misery.

(III, ii, 46–58)

The striking image of the 'plague-sore that would fright a country' reinforces the theme of a hidden evil beneath the outward appearance of virtue and reminds the audience of the self-deception in all of Leantio's claims to goodness. This is the condition not only of his misery, but of all the others, of humanity at large.

Livia, who keeps a 'shop in cunning' (II, ii, 29), will buy the body of Leantio for which she lusts: 'I have enough to buy me my desires' (III, ii, 63). She will 'follow my true labour day by day' (III, ii, 141), a tradesman in sin like Leantio, and it is fitting to the theme that he should sell himself to her for the worldly goods she offers: 'Troth, then, I'll love enough, and take enough' (III, ii, 376). After his sordid bargain, Leantio 'eats his meat with grudging still' (IV, i, 115), while Livia,

Yet, blinded with her appetite, wastes her wealth,
Buys her disgraces at a dearer rate
Than bounteous housekeepers purchase their honour.

(IV, i, 154–6)

Leantio's relation to Livia, like that to Bianca, is expressed by the dramatist in the same terms of food and commerce, and we are left with the feeling that there is no real difference between the two relations, the lustful infatuation of Leantio for the Bianca he has stolen being recapitulated in Livia's lustful infatuation for the Leantio she has bought. Leantio's entire career is cast as a dramatic symbol of dedication to shoddy values which must culminate in his ignominious death.

Bianca too at the beginning of the play prides herself on her virtue, her ability to forego wealth and luxury in dedication to the love of her husband, but it is only the appearance of virtue which she values, and when she is faced with her choice between poverty as a faithful wife and luxury as the Duke's mistress, it is the Duke she chooses. Her seduction, with her feeble attempts at resistance, is an elaborate game, which is emphasized by the parallel game of chess which is played below while it is taking place. The chess game serves to emphasize the essential falseness of Bianca's protestations of chastity, to show that the protests are part of the game and that it is merely the appearance of virtue she is striving to protect. The seduction also is portrayed in commercial terms. 'Why should you seek, sir,' she asks, 'To take away that you can never give' (II, ii, 373-4), and the Duke replies:

> But I give better in exchange - wealth, honour . . .
> Come, play the wise wench, and provide forever;
> Let storms come when they list, they find thee shelter'd.
> Should any doubt arise, let nothing trouble thee;
> Put trust in our love for the managing
> Of all to thy heart's peace: we'll walk together,
> And show a thankful joy for both our fortunes.
>
> (II, ii, 375-92)

The emphasis is upon wealth, security, fortune, and these are covered by the transparent mask of love and honour. Walking out together, Bianca and the Duke are united in a common dedication to lust, but they find their hearts' peace in the delusion that it is love which joins them. Bianca accepts the Duke's values because they are hers as well. Guardiano explains how he had 'to prepare her stomach by degrees / To Cupid's feast' (II, ii, 406-7), the food imagery uniting this faulty moral choice to the others in the play.

Bianco does not regret her corruption, but she turns against Guardiano who has betrayed her:

> sin and I'm acquainted,
> No couple greater; and I'm like that great one,
> Who making politic use of a base villain,
> He likes the treason well, but hates the traitor.
>
> (II, ii, 445-8)

These lines would have a familiar ring to the Jacobean audience, for Bianca is repeating a stock formula of 'Machiavellian policy', that anathema of the age which had become stereotyped in stage tradition. The evil-doer, maintaining always the guise of virtue, must destroy his own evil instrument. The keynote of 'policy' was a seeming virtue as the mask for villainy, and this speech would remind the audience that Bianca's supposed honour is indeed 'leprous' (II, ii, 429), that like Leantio she stands only for a shallow pretence of virtue.

Guardiano accepts the role of villain in images of greed and feeding which link his function as pander to the Duke to the other sordid relations of the play:

> Well, so the Duke love me,
> I fare not much amiss then; two great feasts
> Do seldom come together in one day.
>
> (II, ii, 449–51)

Livia sums up her own role in the seduction of Bianca in much the same poetic terms:

> Sin tastes at first draught like Wormwood water,
> But drunk again, 'tis nectar ever after.
>
> (II, ii, 481–2)

Thus by iterative imagery Middleton links the moral positions of his various characters. All work out their own destruction by making moral commitments, the sordid nature of which is made clear by imagery drawn from money and gluttony. None of these characters is aware of the damnation implicit in his choice of evil, for each of them, like Beatrice-Joanna, prides himself upon his wisdom and prudence. Their initial commitments to evil make them incapable of any other choice than that which must assure their own damnation.

Just as Leantio's sense of loss turns to exultation in the new found wealth of Livia, Bianca's corruption is signalized by a desire for the material objects of wealth:

> some fair cut-work pinned up in my bed chamber,
> A silver and gilt casting-bottle hung by't –
> . . . a silver basin and ewer.
>
> (III, i, 20–23)

She asserts her claim to these paltry objects again in commercial terms: 'And by that copy, this land still I hold' (III, i, 59). Husband and wife together reach the full depth of their degradation as they vaunt their ill-gotten wealth before one another in a kind of ritual dance, each parading the signs of his damnation (IV, i, 42–105). By this scene of symbolic ritual, emphasized by the short clipped speeches with which Bianca and Leantio echo and mock one another, Middleton underscores the theme of his play.

The Duke's moral choice is presented to him by his brother, the Cardinal, who reminds him of the damnation which must be the price of his lechery. The Duke too will preserve the appearance of virtue, committing the greater sins so as to preserve the mere semblance of a virtue he knows he has already forfeited. He will murder the husband so that he can lawfully marry his concubine, desecrating the institution of marriage by making it the license for lust. His marriage to Bianca is the play's culminating instance of moral equivocation, 'religious honours done to sin'(IV, iii, 1–2). The outward signs of holiness mark only an inner corruption, as the Cardinal makes clear:

> Must marriage, that immaculate robe of honour,
> That renders virtue glorious, fair, and fruitful
> To her great master, be now made the garment
> Of leprosy and foulness? Is this penitence
> To sanctify hot lust. What is it otherwise
> Than worship done to devils?
>
> (IV, iii, 13–18)

The clothing image emphasizes once more the deification of false appearance which the marriage will represent, the cloaking of evil with a mask of virtue, which is so dominant a theme in the play. This final sacrilege is linked to the others by another image of loathsome gluttony:

> As if a drunkard, to appease Heaven's wrath,
> Should offer up his surfeit for a sacrifice.
>
> (IV, iii, 21–22)

The seeming health of the Duke, like that of Leantio, hides 'a plague-sore that would fright a country'.

In the sub-plot the moral equivocation of Isabella and Hippolito parallels that of Bianca and the Duke, with the shocking viciousness of the simple-minded Ward to throw into relief the equally cuckolded Leantio. Hippolito and Isabella pride themselves on the nobility of their love, as opposed to the crude commercialism of marriage for which Fabricio stands. They will not commit incest, but they will commit adultery, and Isabella will joy in the knowledge of her supposed bastardy which enables her fully to accept the incestuous relationship she is seeking to avoid. He wisdom is of the same order as that of Beatrice-Joanna; it succeeds only in bringing her to the very damnation she seeks to avoid. Isabella will sell herself to the Ward whom she loathes, and she will accept the very commercial values of her father to which she had once opposed her love for Hippolito. Like Bianca and Leantio, the lovers of the sub-plot willingly commit evil so as to avoid the mere appearance of evil.

This is emphasized further by Hippolito's determination to murder Leantio in order to preserve the appearance of an honour which he knows that he and his sister, Livia, already have forfeited:

> Put case one must be vicious, as I know myself
> Monstrously guilty, there's a blind time made for't,
> He might use only that, – 'twere conscionable;
> Art, silence, closeness, subtlety and darkness,
> Are fit for such a business; but there's no pity
> To be bestowed on an apparent sinner,
> An impudent daylight lecher.
>
> (IV, ii, 5–10)

And he puts his desire for revenge, appropriately to the theme of the play, in terms of wealth and material advantage:

> The great zeal
> I bear to her advancement in this match
> With Lord Vicentio, as the Duke has wrought it
> To the perpetual honour of our house.
>
> (IV, ii, 11–14)

This shallow worship of a meaningless outward appearance is echoed in the comic badinage of the Ward and Sordido. Of the Ward's 'foul skin' Sordido says, 'But you've a clean shirt, and that makes amends, sir' (II, ii, 129–30). Only the outward appearance is valued, no matter what evil lie beneath it. *Women Beware Women* has been criticized as verging too close upon the comic to be truly a tragedy, but the antics of the Ward and his man are bitter comedy, and they are carefully linked to the more serious level of the play so as to support the thematic impact of the whole. The open viciousness of the Ward emphasizes the hidden viciousness of the other characters, for he is linked to them by parallels of action and by a common poetic idiom. When, for instance, with his trapstick the Ward has struck the child of a poulterer's wife, raising 'a bump in her child's head as big as an egg' (I, ii, 96–97) this bit of wanton cruelty is related to the sins of the major characters by the same commercial imagery we have noted:

> An egg may prove a chicken, then in time
> The poulterer's wife will get by't.
>
> (I, ii, 98–99)

In his idiotic tom-foolery the Ward emphasizes the lust, vice and crass commercialism of the major characters, as Sordido details the qualities necessary to the wife he would purchase (II, ii, 103–21), and as they put Isabella through her paces as they would a horse (III, iii).

Such comic commentary links the sub-plot to the main plot, and the common theme of both is made striking by the same poetic imagery. Livia, who at first would defend Isabella from the sordid commercialism of her father, in her earliest speeches puts the relation of women to men in terms of the kitchen:

> Besides, he tastes of many sundry dishes
> That we poor wretches never lay our lips to,
> As obedience forsooth, subjection, duty and such kickshaws,
> All of our making, but serv'd in to them;
> And if we lick a finger then sometimes,
> We're not to blame, your best cooks often use it.
>
> (I, ii, 40–45)

By this use of imagery Middleton prevents his audience from the natural sympathy for Livia which might arise from her seeming opposition to Fabricio's sordid plans. We are made at once aware that she lives in the same moral climate as her brother and that her values are no different from his. We are prepared to see her total villainy emerge at the beginning of the next act.

Hippolito seeks always the outward signs of virtue, but he sums up an important theme of the play in his awareness of the corruption man may carry within himself in spite of outward appearance. He has accepted his incestuous love affair 'even as easily / As man comes by destruction, which ofttimes / He wears in his own bosom' (II, i, 2–4). Like Beatrice-Joanna he can never escape the damnation he carries always within him. Livia offers

her aid in his illicit suit, his 'ill husbandry' (II, i, 13), in terms of
commercial exchange which again link them both to the moral
values of Fabricio to which at their first appearance they had
seemed opposed:

> Thou keep'st the treasure of that life I love
> As dearly as mine own; and if you think
> My former words too bitter, which were minister'd
> By truth and zeal, 'tis but a hazardizing
> Of grace and virtue, and I can bring forth
> As pleasant fruits as sensuality wishes
> In all her teeming longings.

(II, i, 26–32)

Isabella's commitment to sin is linked to that of the other
characters also by the imagery of her lines. Marriage for her is a
relation in which 'women buy their masters' (I, ii, 78), and when
Livia betrays her into her affair with Hippolito, she does so again
in terms of eating:

> If you can make shift here to taste your happiness,
> Or pick out aught that likes you, much good do you;
> You see your cheer, I'll make you no set dinner.

(II, i, 121–3)

When she has tasted Livia's sinful repast, Isabella invites Hippolito to feast upon her love, as she tries to make amends for the
rebuke with which she at first had rejected him:

> When we invite our best friends to a feast,
> 'Tis not all sweetmeats that we set before them;
> There's somewhat sharp and salt, both to whet appetite
> And make 'em taste their wine well; so methinks,
> After a friendly, sharp and savoury chiding,
> A kiss tastes wondrous well, and full o' the grape;
> How think'st thou? does't not?

(II, ii, 198–204)

She describes the secrecy and deception with which they must
conduct their affair in the same poetic terms:

> She that comes once to be a housekeeper
> Must not look every day to fare well, sir,
> Like a young waiting-gentlewoman in service,
> For she feeds commonly as her lady does,

No good bit passes her but she gets a taste on't;
But when she comes to keep house for herself,
She's glad of some choice cates then once a-week,
Or twice at most, and glad if she can get 'em;
So must affection learn to fare with thankfulness.

(II, i, 217–25)

The imagery of these lines makes it impossible for the audience to see the relation of Isabella and Hippolito with any romantic colouring. These lovers do not really decline in moral stature; they are corrupt from the very beginning. They merely become aware of their own corruption as they come to suffer the inevitable tragic consequences.

Except for the role of Livia in both, the main plot and the sub-plot are kept apart until the beginning of the third act. It is significant that they are brought together at a feast at Livia's house. Here the Duke displays Bianca to the world as his concubine, and here the match of Isabella to the Ward is concluded, while in the ironic asides of Leantio and Hippolito the parallel between the two plots is made clear to the audience. It is fitting also that the final climactic scene, with the self-destruction of all the major participants in the formal ritual of a masque, should take place also at a feast, this time in the palace of the Duke. This final scene is utterly without logic in terms of human probability, but the moral choices of which it is the inevitable result have been equally in defiance of logic. The play is unified not in terms of the logic of event or the consistency of character – although there are few figures in Jacobean drama who exhibit the illusion of reality so fully as Leantio and Bianca – but in terms of the larger theme which governs the total play. The final scene is a climactic explosion which the audience experiences as the inevitable result of the moral ambiguities in which the characters have engaged, and of the passions of jealousy, hatred and revenge which these inevitably have engendered. Death is the inevitable end, and the audience is conditioned for the final destruction by the imagery of light and darkness which begins to intrude into the last two acts. In the rapidly moving action of the theatre, the audience, conditioned by the poetry of the lines, does not ask questions of logical probability.

It does no justice to Middleton's art to call him, as T. S. Eliot has done,[1] an author with 'no point of view' whose greatness consists only in the gripping realism of his characterization and of certain scenes. Of his realism there can be no doubt, but he is also a highly moralistic artist who could skilfully pattern his action in terms of a central theme. His scenes are often ritualistic and symbolic, and his poetic language is carefully chosen as the instrument by which the parts of his play are related to one another. *Women Beware Women*, like *The Changeling*, is a unified work of art governed by a moral point of view to which all of the parts contribute.

[1] *Selected Essays*, p. 162.

CHAPTER SEVEN

John Ford

I

In a widely influential essay written some half century ago, Stuart P. Sherman set the pattern which has shaped most subsequent criticism of John Ford.[1] Sherman called Ford a 'decadent' dramatist, the last writer of tragedy in tragedy's greatest age, whose plays came as a sterile anti-climax to the great achievements of Shakespeare, Marlowe and Webster. He saw Ford as the romantic apostle of illicit love who could glorify even incest for the delight of an effete upper class audience, sated with the ordinary fare of a drama whose novelty had long been exhausted. Ford for Sherman stood for moral anarchy; interested only in shocking the moral sense of his audience he made sin appear beautiful and thus created a kind of problem play which implicitly denied all moral order.

Sherman's views have been subject to some questioning in recent years,[2] but Ford is still generally regarded as one who, if not immoral himself, deliberately avoided the great moral issues of his age. He has been called a psychologist interested only in the complexities of individual behaviour, 'in any situation that revealed character, normal as well as abnormal, and in characters conventionally moral or immoral.'[3] One writer sees Ford's

[1] 'Forde's Contribution to the Decadence of the Drama,' in *John Fordes Dramatische Werke*, ed. W. Bang, *Materialen zur Kunde des alteren Englischen Dramas*, XXIII (Louvain, 1908).
[2] See M. E. Prior, *The Language of Tragedy*, p. 145. H. J. Oliver, *The Problem of John Ford* (Melbourne, 1955), goes to the opposite extreme in seeing Ford as a champion of the conventional moral order. Other attempts to find a conventional morality in Ford's plays include G. H. Blayney, 'Convention, Plot and Structure in "The Broken Heart",' *MP*, LVI (1958), 1–9; Cyrus Hoy, 'Ignorance in Knowledge: Marlowe's Faustus and Ford's Giovanni,' *MP*, LVII (1960), 145–54, and very notably, Ornstein, *The Moral Vision*, pp. 200–1, who writes that Ford 'presents the rare individual instance that proves conventional moral generalizations' (p. 212).
[3] M. Joan Sargeaunt, *John Ford* (Oxford, 1935), p. 140. See also Una M. Ellis-Fermor, *The Jacobean Drama*, pp. 225–46.

characters primarily as clinical case-studies based upon Burton's *Anatomy of Melancholy*, and calls Ford a scientific determinist who 'removes human activity from the realm of ethical choice, and anticipating the exponents of modern thought, looks at life with amoral eyes'.[1] T. S. Eliot has called Ford a dramatist without purpose and *'Tis Pity* a failure because it does not 'dramatize an action or struggle for harmony in the soul of the poet',[2] and Clifford Leech offers no explanation in moral terms for the suffering which Ford's characters have learned to accept with stoic dignity and without question in a world in which 'vicissitude has become irrelevant'.[3]

I would suggest that Ford struggled as fully as his predecessors had struggled with the problem of man's position in the universe. He is, in fact, among the most obvious of writers in his moral concern, but his moral position is more subtle than his critics usually have been willing to allow. Ford does not hold up incest or illicit love for the admiration of his audience; he is not a champion of moral anarchy, but it is nevertheless true that he arouses a pity for the incestuous lovers of *'Tis Pity* such as Middleton never does for those of *Women Beware Women*: this is implicit in the words of Giovanni before he kills Annabella:

> Kiss me; if ever after times should hear
> Of our fast-knit affections, though perhaps
> The laws of conscience and of civil use
> May justly blame us, yet when they but know
> Our loves, that love will wipe away that rigour
> Which would in other incests be abhorred.
>
> (2380–5)

This is not a defence of incest, but it is a plea for sympathy for the lovers on the basis of a natural human feeling which we can

---

[1] G. F. Sensabaugh, *The Tragic Muse of John Ford* (Palo Alto, Calif., 1944), p. 70. On the influence of Burton, see also S. Blaine Ewing, *Burtonian Melancholy in the Plays of John Ford* (Princeton, 1940).

[2] *Selected Essays*, p. 196. Cf. also M. C. Bradbrook, *Themes and Conventions*, pp. 250–261, who sees Ford as a mere imitator of his predecessors, writing with no real underlying purpose.

[3] *John Ford and the Drama of his Time* (London, 1957), particularly p. 74. Robert Davril, in the most comprehensive of recent works on Ford, *Le Drame de John Ford* (Paris, 1954) sees in the plays also a stoic acceptance of suffering in a world which can no longer accept traditional values.

understand, and it is an exposure of the ordinary limitations of 'the laws of conscience and of civil use'. What sets Ford apart from his contemporaries is not a disregard for moral issues, but an inability to lead his audience to a full resolution of the moral problems which he poses. His are the tragedies of paradox, products of a sceptical age which can no longer accept without question the doctrine of a human law reflecting the will of God in a perfectly reasonable and harmonious universe, such as Richard Hooker had expressed it in some half century before. We cannot find in Ford's tragedies the kind of moral certainty we may find in Shakespeare, and it is this fact which reveals John Ford as among the most pessimistic tragedians of his age. He draws for us the tragic plight of humanity aware always of evil but unable to find good, forced to live in a world where moral certainty seems impossible, and able to escape destruction only by blind conformity to principles which oppose man's reason and his most basic human feelings. The tragedy of Ford's heroes and heroines is in their inability to find a satisfactory alternative to sin. They can only die with courage and dignity.

Although Ford appears to have been writing for the stage as early as 1621 when he shared in the composition of *The Witch of Edmonton*, his particular contribution to English tragedy may be summed up by four plays of the following decade. *'Tis Pity She's A Whore*, *Love's Sacrifice* and *The Broken Heart* were all published in 1633, and *Perkin Warbeck* followed in 1634. It has usually been assumed that *'Tis Pity* was the earliest of these plays, largely on the basis of Ford's reference to the play in his dedication to the Earl of Peterborough as 'These *first fruits of my leisure*'. Such an assumption, however, is hardly warranted, for Ford's statement is, to say the least, extremely ambiguous.[1] We have no real evidence as to either the dates of Ford's four masterpieces or the order of their composition. I do believe, however, that the play in which Ford's particular tragic position most clearly and forcefully emerges is *'Tis Pity She's A Whore*, and I would tend to regard this play as the culmination of a movement begun in *The Broken Heart* and continued in *Love's Sacrifice*. As a history

[1] See G. E. Bentley, *The Jacobean and Caroline Stage*, III, 436–7, 440–2, 451–6, 462–4, for the most thorough survey of the chronology problems.

play, *Perkin Warbeck* stands somewhat apart from the others, but if I were forced to hazard a time of composition, I would place it immediately after *'Tis Pity She's A Whore*.

II

There is a unity of tone in *The Broken Heart* and what Professor Ellis-Fermor has called a quality of stillness.[1] Although the play is full of suffering, violence and death, we do not feel the turbulence of passion; there is a calm about the action, emphasized most strongly in the dignified and studied death of Calantha at the end, and we seem to see the characters as figures in a dream. In this unique quality the play's greatness lies, for in spite of its somewhat overburdened plot, it is a unified aesthetic whole. But in this quality is also the play's weakness as tragedy, for it induces a sense of detachment which makes it difficult for us to feel the vitality and significance of the moral issues the play poses. The influence of Beaumont and Fletcher is strong – it is natural that Ford should have begun by imitating the dominant tragic mode of his day – and it lends a note of artificiality which renders *The Broken Heart* a far less moving work than *'Tis Pity*, where Ford seems to have broken entirely from the Beaumont and Fletcher tradition and found his own tragic style.

The setting of *The Broken Heart* in a mythical Sparta reminiscent of Sidney's *Arcadia*, and the pastoral names of the characters contribute to the play's artificiality. The influence of Beaumont and Fletcher is seen also in that the play's moral issues involve the same kind of conflict of absolutes we may find in their plays, with characters incapable of varying from an initially determined moral stance.[2] But Ford goes beyond his models in that whereas the conflicts in Beaumont and Fletcher are usually resolved by artificially contrived action – such as Evadne's killing the king in *The Maid's Tragedy* – which avoid the moral issues and leave the conflicting absolutes undisturbed, Ford's conflicts cannot be resolved, and if they also are based upon the conflicting demands

[1] *The Jacobean Drama*, pp. 236–7. See also Leech, p. 75 ff., who sees the movement in Ford's tragedies towards the moment of stillness, the static scene, which he sees most perfectly realized in *The Broken Heart*.

[2] See J. F. Danby, *Poets on Fortune's Hill* (London, 1952), pp. 152–206.

of absolute codes of social behaviour, they are made to reflect upon the larger problem which is always Ford's concern: man's inability to find his place in the universe.

There is no active force of evil in *The Broken Heart*. All of the characters are exemplary in their virtue, and they are caught in the consequences of an act belonging to the past, irrevocable and beyond human control. The disposal by Ithocles of his sister Penthea to Bassanes is the root of all the play's difficulties, but this has taken place long before the opening of the action. Ithocles himself regrets it as the action of a hasty and irresponsible youth he has left behind him. He is no longer the man who committed the act; that man no longer exists. This placing of evil's origins outside the sphere of the play's action creates a feeling of fatalism somewhat similar to that of Shakespeare's *Romeo and Juliet* where the young lovers step into a world already full of an ancient evil not of their own creation. There is a difference, however, in that the world of *Romeo and Juliet* affords a means for evil's extinction, whereas that of *The Broken Heart* does not. Ford exhibits only the heroic suffering and the calm and dignified death of men and women who cannot excape the demands of conflicting moral commitments.

Of this human plight Penthea is Ford's supreme example. She seeks only for virtue in terms of an inexorable moral law, but her very pursuit of virtue involves her more and more deeply in sin; to be faithful to her husband, Bassanes, she must be a whore to Orgilus, to whom she has been married in spirit:

> For she that's wife to Orgilus, and lives
> In known adultery with Bassanes,
> Is at best a whore.
>
> (1200–2)

There is no escape but death, and in her death speech she points to the tragic paradox which has destroyed her:

> Oh my wrack'd honour ruin'd by those tyrants,
> A cruel brother and a desperate dotage!
> There is no peace left for a ravish'd wife
> Widow'd by lawless marriage; to all memory,
> Penthea's, poor Penthea's name is strumpeted.
>
> (1951–5)

The woman who has pursued honour and made an ideal of chastity to the extent of destroying both herself and the man she truly loves dies a whore in spite of all. To preserve the honour of her husband in name she must destroy that of her husband in spirit. Her pursuit of virtue not only negates the normal feelings of humanity but makes a mockery of virtue itself. She is the slave of a moral position into which she has been thrust by an action over which she has had no control.

The fate of Penthea serves as a dramatic symbol of the uncertainty of all human values. Those absolutes which men most firmly revere, love, friendship, honour, may be the very sources of hatred, death and desecration. In Penthea's honesty is her whoredom; in her fidelity to Bassanes is her betrayal of Orgilus. There is even the suggestion that the jealousy of Bassanes springs from what is good, the beauty of Penthea and his reverence for that beauty:

> Bassanes
> The man that calls her wife; considers truly
> What heaven of perfections he is lord of,
> By thinking fair Penthea his. This thought
> Begets a kind of monster love, which love
> Is nurse unto a fear so strong and servile,
> As brands all dotage with a jealousy.
>
> (148–54)

Thus beauty becomes the source of its own destruction. There is no certainty of good of any kind in *The Broken Heart*, only the conflict of commitments to social codes which at last seem arbitrary and without meaning.

Such is the force which guides Orgilus. Just as Penthea is destroyed by her ideal of chastity and fidelity in marriage, Orgilus is destroyed by his own code of honour. His betrothed has been taken away from him by Ithocles who thus has become the destroyer of his honour. Honour demands revenge, but Orgilus has come to love and admire Ithocles, and vengeance thus demands the destruction of his friend. That the Euphranea-Prophilus relationship is not adequately developed is a flaw in the play, but from what we do have of it, it appears that in having Orgilus assert control over his sister's marriage, Ford may have intended

a further illustration of the paradox implicit in Orgilus's position.
To avenge himself against Ithocles he must prevent the marriage
of his sister to the friend of Ithocles, but in doing so he must
destroy his own sister just as Penthea has been destroyed by her
brother, Ithocles. To avenge the sin against himself he must
become as guilty as the sinner he opposes. That Orgilus at last
gives his consent to his sister's marriage is a weakness in the play,
for it lessens the emphasis upon this moral paradox and it renders
Euphranea and Prophilus somewhat extraneous to the central
action, although Ford may have been trying to use these lovers as
an illustration of what Penthea and Orgilus might have been and
thus to heighten the pathos of their destruction.

The paradox in Orgilus's position is implicit in the means of
Ithocles's death. Orgilus must kill the friend he admires because
honour demands it, but the manner of the killing involves a total
forfeit of honour, for Orgilus stabs Ithocles while he is trapped by
the 'engine' which renders him powerless. In killing Ithocles
basely, Orgilus denies the honour he has been seeking to preserve.
The device of the 'engine' is not, as is so often supposed, merely
an instance of Ford's catering to the demands of his audience for
the bizarre and sensational. It is crucial to the theme of the play,
as Orgilus makes clear at the end:

> Nor did I use an engine to entrap
> His life out of a slavish fear to combat
> Youth, strength, or cunning, but for that I durst not
> Engage the goodness of a cause on fortune,
> By which his name might have outfac'd my vengeance:
> Oh Tecnicus, inspir'd with Phoebus' fire,
> I call to mind thy augury, 'twas perfect;
> Revenge proves its own executioner.
>
> (2489-96)

The demands of vengeance could only be safely met by an abdica-
tion of those very premisses of honour which had dictated vengeance in the first place. Honour for Orgilus has been the destroyer
of honour as it has been the destroyer of life; revenge has been
its own executioner.

Tecnicus is used to offer an ideal of honour against which the
actions of the other characters may be measured:

Honour consists not in a bare opinion
By doing any act that feeds content;
Brave in appearance, 'cause we think it brave:
Such honour comes by accident, not nature
Proceeding from the vices of our passion
Which makes our reason drunk. But real honour
Is the reward of virtue, and acquir'd
By justice or by valour, which for basis
Hath justice to uphold it. He then fails
In honour, who for lucre or revenge
Commits thefts, murders, treasons and adulteries,
With such like, by intrenching on just laws,
Whose sov'reignty is best preserv'd by justice.
Thus as you see how honour must be grounded
On knowledge, not opinion: For opinion
Relies on probability and accident,
But knowledge on necessity and truth:
I leave thee to the fit consideration
Of what becomes the grace of real honour,
Wishing success to all thy virtuous meanings.

(1070–89)

The philosopher is predicting what Orgilus is to experience: that an honour based on the uncertain values of the social order (opinion) must be its own destruction, and that true honour must be based upon the kind of moral certainty (knowledge) which none of the characters of *The Broken Heart* is capable of attaining.

The grim fatalism of the play is emphasized in the plight of Ithocles, the prisoner of his own past, enslaved in his maturity by

the heat
Of an unsteady youth, a giddy brain,
Green indiscretion, flattery of greatness,
Rawness of judgment, wilfulness in folly,
Thoughts vagrant as the wind, and as uncertain,
Might lead a boy in years to.

(775–80)

Ithocles must suffer the consequences of a course of action which once set in motion cannot be averted; there is no room in Ford's world for divine forgiveness or reconciliation. The tragedy of

Ithocles is that of man's inability to atone for sin; his penance is of no avail:

> I now repent it;
> Now, uncle, now; this 'now', is now too late:
> So provident is folly in sad issue,
> That after-wit, like bankrupts' debts, stand tallied
> Without all possibilities of payment.
>
> (1646–9)

Ithocles is the prisoner not only of the folly of his own youth, but also of a rigid social code which makes it impossible for him to express his love for the princess, Calantha. He mirrors the general plight of man in his helpless suffering, and he serves as a model for what to Ford is the only glory of which man is capable, the calmness and courage with which he dies.

There are four kinds of suffering in *The Broken Heart*: that of Orgilus through his own pursuit of vengeance, that of Ithocles because of his own past action, that of Penthea through another's act directed against her, and finally that of Calantha as the final victim of a series of events begun by others and with little relation to her own concerns. She is a poignant example of that human suffering which Ford sees in the very nature of things, a suffering which need not be attributed either to one's own act or to the malice of any external agent. Calantha's tragedy is utterly without human cause or reason. Her death scene, so often condemned as mere theatrical sensationalism, is Ford's most dramatic means of showing man's only answer to such suffering. Calantha dies with a studied calm and dignity, performing all of the necessary duties of life before she goes. We have as the final statement of the play the inability of man to avoid suffering and death, with his destruction implicit in moral paradoxes which he cannot resolve. The only good he can seek is in a calm, fearless recognition of this human plight, in a stoic devotion to duty and in an acceptance of death with courage and dignity. In spite of its artificial setting and its many dramatic flaws, *The Broken Heart* is the vehicle for a tragic view of life.

What *The Broken Heart* lacks is the kind of emotional intensity which may enable an audience to experience fully the tragic vision it unfolds. This intensity Ford achieved in *'Tis Pity She's A Whore*, and we may perceive some movement towards it in *Love's Sacrifice*, for this play does place its characters in the real world of Renaissance Italy, although the moral paradoxes which destroy them spring from a particular neo-platonic love code as far removed from reality as the code of honour in *The Broken Heart*.[1] We do not have in *Love's Sacrifice* characters of an inflexible and unalterable virtue. Now they are subject to ordinary human passions and temptations which serve to humanize them and which permit the audience more fully to participate in their disasters. In the machinations of D'Avalos and Fiormunda, moreover, Ford makes his audience aware of evil as it never is in *The Broken Heart*. If the Ferrentes sub-plot of *Love's Sacrifice* has any function, it is to reinforce for the audience this sense of evil's reality and omnipresence.

For these reasons I would regard *Love's Sacrifice* as a movement towards the kind of tragedy Ford realized in *'Tis Pity She's A Whore*. Otherwise, *Love's Sacrifice* is the least successful of Ford's tragedies, for it has none of the excellence which stems from the very artificiality of *The Broken Heart*, its particular unity of tone. The plot is as overloaded as that of *The Broken Heart*, with such large elements as the banishment and disguise of Roseilli very difficult to relate to the rest of the play, and with the comedy of Mauruccio and Giacopo neither amusing nor in keeping with the rest. What remains when all of the extraneous matter in *Love's Sacrifice* is ignored is the central poignant situation of Bianca who loves Fernando with a physical passion she cannot overcome in spite of all the forces of society which demand her fidelity to the kind and benevolent Duke who has taken her without dowry to be his duchess; while Fernando is torn between his own physical passion for Bianca and his friendship for the Duke. We approach the theme of *'Tis Pity She's A Whore* in this play, for *Love's Sacrifice* concentrates also upon the conflict between man's obedience to his own human impulses and his need to conform to a social order which runs counter to them. Man is a slave both of his own physical being and of the society into which he is born;

---

[1] Peter Ure, 'Cult and Initiates in Love's Sacrifice,' *MLQ*, XI (1951), 298–306, sees the tragedy as that of Bianca, the would-be adultress whose physical nature makes her incapable of living up to a neo-platonic code of love, as Fernando does.

over neither has he had any control. He is destroyed by their conflicting demands, and he has no escape other than in the courage of his death.

III

When we turn to *'Tis Pity She's A Whore*, we leave the dream world of Beaumont and Fletcher with its artificial standards of virtue and its elaborate social codes. We enter the world of Webster and Marston, Renaissance Italy, full of intrigue and of an evil which is as pervasive as it is real. In *'Tis Pity* Ford poses the moral paradoxes of the earlier plays in more realistic terms, in a setting we can experience as true, and in characters with whom we can emotionally identify ourselves. As in the other plays, death is the only resolution to the moral conflicts of *'Tis Pity*; no real ideal of virtue is possible for man. But the impossibility of good makes all the more striking the reality of evil which in this play Ford displays more fully than in any other of his plays.

Giovanni and Annabella are transgressors; their sins are destructive both of society and human life. The bleeding heart on Giovanni's dagger is a poignant symbol of the desecration of life to which their conduct must lead. For their sins they suffer and they die, but while Ford shows us the fruits of such transgression, he does not defend the moral order against which they transgress. By the use of his carefully linked sub-plots Ford shows the woeful inadequacy of the very human and divine institutions by which Giovanni and Annabella are condemned and destroyed. The peculiar tension of *'Tis Pity* springs from Ford's inability to offer any real alternative to sin. The final statement of the play is that man must conform to a moral order whose inadequacy he always knows, for the only escape from moral uncertainty lies in desecration and death. That such uncertainty is the necessary condition of man is established in the opening lines of the play:

> Dispute no more in this, for know (young man)
> These are no school-points; nice philosophy
> May tolerate unlikely arguments,
> But Heaven admits no jest; wits that presum'd
> On wit too much, by striving how to prove
> There was no God, with foolish grounds of art,

> Discover'd first the nearest way to hell;
> And filled the world with devilish atheism:
> Such questions, youth, are fond; for better 'tis
> To bless the sun, than reason why it shines.
>
> (55-65)

The Friar draws a distinction between rational philosophy and revealed religion; he urges a blind acceptance in spite of reason.[1] Accept without question, the Friar urges, while the action displays the sordidness of what must be accepted. The tragedy of Giovanni is that he cannot accept blindly, and in the quest for certainty lies inevitable destruction. Giovanni is the philosopher,

> that miracle of wit
> Who once within these three months wert esteem'd
> A wonder of thine age throughout Bononia?
> How did the university applaud
> Thy government, behaviour, learning, speech,
> Sweetness, and all that could make up a man.
>
> (105-10)

He is man in his highest state of excellence, reflected in the beauty of his physical form, man the seeker after truth, and it is his very need to know which is his destruction. ' 'Tis not I know, / My lust; but 'tis my fate that leads me on' (308-9), he says in an important soliloquy. This fate which destroys him is in his very nature as a sentient and intelligent man.

The sub-plots are related to one another and controlled by the governing theme of the play in that each one is designed to make clear some aspect of the moral order which Giovanni cannot blindly accept. The Cardinal is needed to pass religion's judgment upon Giovanni at the end, but the corruption of this very religion is at the same time made apparent:

> And all the gold and jewels, or whatsoever,
> Confiscate by the canons of the church,
> We seize upon to the Pope's proper use.
>
> (2588-90)

---

[1] Sargeaunt, *John Ford*, pp. 124-5, holds that this blind acceptance in defiance of formal philosophy, 'in spite of Thomas Aquinas, accords with much of the theology of the Medieval church.' Miss Sargeaunt, however, finds the Friar an 'enigma', entirely inconsistent in his religious position: 'When he gives his blessing to the marriage feast one feels that he must be either a complete knave or a complete fool' (p. 126). I would regard the Friar's confused religious position as part of Ford's deliberate purpose, his means of showing religion's inadequacy.

It had been made clear earlier by his protection of the murderer Grimaldi and by the moral equivocation of Friar Bonaventura. The institutions of courtship and marriage and society's code of honour are represented by Soranzo, with the Hippolita sub-plot to throw them into relief. Two aspects of justice are displayed: the corruption of divine law in the exoneration of Grimaldi, and the painful futility of earthly vengeance in the intrigues of Richardetto. The ideals of true service and loyalty are rendered sordid by Vasques and Putana. The fool, Bergetto and his man are used to throw these themes into sharper focus. His courtship of Annabella makes ludicrous the role of Florio in the disposition of his daughter according to the customs of the age. The pathos of Bergetto's death makes more poignant the injustice of the Cardinal, and the simple fidelity of Poggio mourning over the body of his master throws the brutal fidelity of Vasques into clearer light. If we admire Giovanni it is not because Ford would glorify incest, but because of the sordidness of the established moral order to which he stands opposed.

The Friar's opening words, as we have seen, affirm the inscrutability of divine law: 'For better 'tis / To bless the sun, than reason why it shines.' This is the staple of his religion and when Giovanni asserts the normal condition of nature (82–92) as justification for incest, the Friar cannot answer his argument; he can only counsel an unquestioning subjection to the ritual of the church:

> then fall down
> On both thy knees, and grovel on the ground:
> Cry to thy heart, wash every word thou utter'st
> In tears, and if't be possible, of blood:
> Beg heaven to cleanse the leprosy of lust
> That rots thy soul, acknowledge what thou art,
> A wretch, a worm, a nothing: weep, sigh, pray
> Three times a day, and three times every night:
> For seven days' space do this.
>
> (129–37)

The Friar's religion involves a debasement of man, a denial of his intellectual capacity, and this Giovanni accepts:

> All this I'll do, to free me from the rod
> Of vengeance, else I'll swear my fate's my God.
>
> (142–3)

He goes through all of the formal ritual of religion, but it offers
him no release, for he cannot deny his own nature as a thinking
man as such religion demands; he must have answers to his questions which the Friar and his religion cannot give.

Ford creates an antithesis between a blind acceptance of the
existing religious and moral order on the one hand, and on the
other an acceptance of fate as man's controlling principle. For
Giovanni to acknowledge the primacy of fate rather than divine
law is for him to see himself as governed not by God but by those
forces which are inherent in his nature as a man. In the very
lines with which he recounts the futility of his attempt to follow
the Friar's advice, Giovanni avows his acceptance of fate, which
is to acknowledge his human condition with all its inevitable
consequences:

> Lost, I am lost: my fates have doomed my death:
> The more I strive, I love, the more I love,
> The less I hope: I see my ruin, certain.
> What judgment, or endeavours could apply
> To my incurable and restless wounds,
> I throughly have examin'd, but in vain:
> O that it were not in religion sin,
> To make our love a god, and worship it.
> I have even wearied heaven with prayers, dried up
> The spring of my continual tears, even starved
> My veins with daily fasts: what wit or art
> Could counsel, I have practised; but alas
> I find all these but dreams and old men's tales
> To fright unsteady youth; I'm still the same,
> Or I must speak, or burst; 'tis not I know
> My lust; but 'tis my fate that leads me on.
>
> (294–309)

When he says to Annabella, 'I have asked counsel of the holy
church, / Who tells me I may love you' (403–4), Giovanni is not
practising a cheap duplicity. He is saying to the audience that
although he has followed the ritual of the church it has offered
him no help; in the inability of religion to convince him of evil,
he finds a justification for evil.

Giovanni constructs his defence of incest out of the very scholastic principles on which the Friar's religion is based:

> What I have done, I'll prove both fit and good.
> It is a principle (which you have taught
> When I was yet your scholar) that the frame
> And composition of the mind doth follow
> The frame and composition of the body:
> So where the body's furniture is beauty,
> The mind's must needs be virtue: which allowed,
> Virtue itself is reason but refin'd,
> And love the quintessence of that; this proves
> My sister's beauty being rarely fair,
> Is rarely virtuous; chiefly in her love,
> And chiefly in that love, her love to me.
> If hers to me, then so is mine to her;
> Since in like causes are effects alike.
>
> (918–31)

This moral casuistry does not represent Ford's point of view. It is a specious parody of scholastic logic designed to emphasize the shallowness of the very moral postulates of the Friar's religion. Giovanni has learned from his religious teacher only how to justify in religion's own terms the shocking perversion of nature which is incest. To this the Friar has no rational answer. He can only again assert that religion must prevail in spite of human reason:

> O ignorance in knowledge, long ago,
> How often have I warn'd thee this before?
> Indeed if we were sure there were no deity,
> Nor heaven nor hell, then to be led alone,
> By nature's light (as were philosophers
> Of elder times) might instance some defence.
> But 'tis not so; then madman, thou wilt find,
> That nature is in heaven's positions blind.
>
> (932–9)

When the Friar urges Giovanni to 'Persuade thy sister to some marriage' (945), his reply is an indictment of the moral system from which this suggestion springs: 'Marriage? Why that's to damn her; that's to prove / Her greedy of variety of lust' (946–7). The retort is shocking, but it states the logical corollary to the

Friar's position, and its truth is borne out by the consequence of Annabella's acceptance of the Friar's religion in a later scene designed perhaps to contrast with her brother's rejection of it.

When Annabella comes before him wringing her hands and weeping in her abject penitence, the Friar draws for her a picture of hell in conventional terms:

> There is a place
> (List daughter) in a black and hollow vault,
> Where day is never seen; there shines no sun,
> But flaming horror of consuming fires;
> A lightless sulphur, choked with smoky fogs
> Of an infected darkness; in this place
> Dwell many thousand, thousand sundry sorts
> Of never dying deaths; there damned souls
> Roar without pity, there are gluttons fed
> With toads and adders; there is burning oil
> Poured down the drunkard's throat, the usurer
> Is forced to sup whole draughts of molten gold;
> There is the murderer forever stabbed,
> Yet can he never die; there lies the wanton
> On racks of burning steel, whiles in his soul
> He feels the torment of his raging lust.
>
> (1406–21)

Annabella in her terror calls 'Mercy, oh mercy' (1422), and when she asks, 'Is there no way left to redeem my miseries?' (1432), the Friar offers the best his religion can afford:

> There is, despair not; heaven is merciful,
> And offers grace even now; 'tis thus agreed,
> First, for your honour's safety that you marry
> The Lord Soranzo, next, to save your soul,
> Leave off this life, and henceforth live to him.
>
> (1433–7)

To earn the grace of heaven she must cheat Soranzo; to save her own honour she must commit the greatest crime against Soranzo's honour of which her society could conceive. The Friar's counsel is, as Giovanni has suggested, that she heap sin upon sin, and we know that when she follows it her tragedy will only be hastened and intensified. The Friar's religion only offers moral equivocation whose shallowness is immediately apparent. Giovanni scorns religion while Annabella seeks it; to neither can it afford any solution.

Ford takes special pains to depict the society which condemns the incestuous lovers, with its code of honour and its standards of nobility, as sordid and self-destructive. 'I am a Roman and a gentleman, one that have got / Mine honour with expense of blood' (159–60), cries Grimaldi when first he appears upon the scene. 'You are a lying coward and a fool' (101), replies Vasques as he beats him down, and in this is Ford's commentary upon the social values for which Grimaldi stands. He is never mentioned without some reference to his high connections and his noble blood, but his nobility can only express itself in the sordid plot of Richardetto, and his sole accomplishment is to stab a pathetic fool. Yet Grimaldi's is the kind of honour which the world respects and which merits the special protection of cardinal and pope.

The shallowness of worldly honour and of the moral sanctions of marriage is made even more clear in the meeting between Soranzo and Hippolita. He has seduced her with promises of marriage, and he has been instrumental in the supposed death of her husband, but now he rejects her claims upon him with a moral sophistry blatant in its hypocrisy:

> The vows I made, if you remember well,
> Were wicked and unlawful; 'twere more sin
> To keep them than to break them; as for me,
> I cannot mask my penitence; think thou
> How much thou hast digressed from honest shame,
> In bringing of a gentleman to death
> Who was thy husband.
>
> (703–9)

Even Vasques is moved to comment, 'This part has been scurvily played' (719), but Soranzo's moral position is that of the very world which condemns Giovanni and Annabella, for there is no secret of Soranzo's past relation to Hippolita, and he is accepted by all as the image of nobility most fit to be Annabella's husband.

The tragedy which falls upon Soranzo is a product of the very moral code for which he stands, for as Annabella tells him, ' 'twas not for love / I chose you, but for honour' (1791-2). The fruits of the very honour which moved her to betray him are made evident as Soranzo drags his wife by the hair across the stage, crying in his torment only for vengeance. His kind of love, with all of the sanctions of honour, religion and social custom, can only express itself in the tormented fury of the cuckold. We see the evil of Giovanni's violation of moral law, but we see also the evil implicit in Soranzo's conformity to it.

In the idea of a harmonious cosmological order which Elizabethans carried over from the Middle Ages, the true servant had an honoured place. In his loyalty to his master he reflected his master's loyalty to his king and his king's loyalty to God. A chain of trust and obedience extended from highest to lowest, cemented by the love of God for man which was reflected in the king's concern for the welfare of his people and the master's care of his servant, who repaid him with true service, loyalty and devotion. Upon this system Ford's Vasques is an ironic reflection. Of his absolute loyalty to Soranzo there is never any question, but this very loyalty is a destructive force in the social order. It fosters the plot of Hippolita and her consequent death, as it is to destroy Giovanni and Annabella and even Soranzo himself. This carnage is the fruit of his loyalty, and in it Vasques exults: 'I have paid the duty to the son, which I have vowed to the father' (2551–2). There is no place for remorse in the system he represents: 'what I have done was duty, and I repent nothing, but that the loss of my life had not ransom'd his' (2559–60).

The very loyalty of Vasques is a sordid commentary upon a social order and a moral system dear to the Elizabethans, but which Ford could not accept in the same unquestioning spirit. _'Tis Pity She's A Whore_ is a product of Caroline scepticism. It opposes to accepted standards of religion and morality the crime of incest, not because Ford approves of this, but because it is probably the most shocking challenge to traditional values of which he can conceive. It is a dramatic symbol of the moral uncertainty which is the theme of the play. Ford is saying that this moral uncertainty which is the fate of thinking man may also be the source of his destruction. Man has no alternative but to accept, difficult as such acceptance may be. The way of Giovanni is evil, but that of Soranzo is not good. Man cannot fully embrace the one position or the other, and in this dilemma is the essence of his tragedy.

Giovanni when he first encounters Annabella in the play is a 'blessed shape / Of some celestial creature' (277–8), and Annabella is the paragon of female beauty, the perfection of their bodies reflecting that of their souls. Ford uses all of his poetic powers to display them as superior in mind and body to the sordid world which must condemn and destroy them. By their very magnificence their tragedy is heightened; the Friar laments that 'one so excellent should give those parts / All to a second death' (965–6). As they defy the moral order which they cannot bring themselves to accept they both disintegrate and become hardened in vice. They often have been compared to Shakespeare's Romeo and Juliet. The crucial difference is that while Shakespeare's young lovers grow to maturity through pain and suffering, Ford's lovers decline from an initial magnificence to the sordid desecration of life implicit in Giovanni's entrance with the bleeding heart upon his sword. But Ford's lovers merit no less of pity and admiration than Shakespeare's, for their tragedy is an heroic opposition of their own humanity to a world which they cannot accept. The price of such opposition must be sin and death, but such self-destruction is not without its heroic quality.

That Giovanni's love for his sister is an assertion of primitive nature in opposition to human and divine law is made clear at the beginning:

> Shall a peevish sound,
> A customary form, from man to man,
> Of brother and of sister, be a bar
> 'Twixt my perpetual happiness and me?
> Say that we had one father, say one womb,
> (Curse to my joys) gave both us life, and birth;
> Are we not therefore each to other bound
> So much the more by Nature; by the links
> Of blood, of reason; Nay if you will hav't,
> Even of religion, to be ever one,
> One soul, one flesh, one love, one heart, one all?
>
> (82-92)

Religion, he is arguing, can have no validity when it runs counter to the claims of nature. He is led, as the Friar exclaims, 'By nature's light as were philosophers / Of elder times,' (936–7).

But the irony is that human reason guided only by the light of nature can lead only to self-deception and error. This is evident in the smug sense of victory with which Giovanni in the final act congratulates himself upon his triumph over the world's morality:

> Busy opinion is an idle fool
> That as a school-rod keeps a child in awe,
> Frights the unexperienced temper of the mind:
> So did it me; who ere my precious sister
> Was married, thought all taste of love would die
> In such a contract; but I find no change
> Of pleasure in this formal law of sports.
> She is still one to me, and every kiss
> As sweet and as delicious as the first
> I reaped, when yet the privilege of youth
> Entitled her a virgin: O the glory
> Of two united hearts like hers and mine!
> Let poring bookmen dream of other worlds,
> My world and all of happiness is here,
> And I'ld not change it for the best to come.
> A life of pleasure is Elysium.
>
> (2145–60)

This is the height of his delusion, rudely to be shattered by the Friar who enters with the news that his incest has been discovered. He has not, after all, been master of the world, but entirely subject to it. His felicity has rested upon a crude deception and subterfuge, subject to destruction by the weak foolishness of a Putana and the perverted loyalty of a Vasques. It can only issue now in his complete degeneration as he murders Annabella, the madness of the act punctuated by her dying words: 'Brother unkind, unkind – mercy great heaven' (2410).

Living by the light of nature alone, Giovanni has become the destroyer of life and of all human value. Of this the heart upon his sword is a dramatic symbol:

> Be not amaz'd; if your misgiving hearts
> Shrink at an idle sight; what bloodless fear
> Of coward passion would have seized your senses,

Had you beheld the rape of life and beauty
Which I have acted?

(2444-8)

He boasts of his final desecration, while he tells the audience in
the imagery of his lines that it has been a perversion of nature:
'The glory of my deed / Darkened the mid-day sun, made noon
as night' (2450-1). He who would live by nature comes at last to
be the destroyer of nature, as he has destroyed his family, 'gilt
in the blood / Of a fair sister and a hapless father' (2504-5). As
he courts his own destruction, he dying acknowledges the feeble-
ness of the human condition: 'Feeble arms / Have you so soon
lost strength' (2521-2).

Ford sees mankind poised, like a morality play hero, between
divine law and a nature which seems in opposition to it; but unlike
the morality hero he is incapable of choice. If human reason will
not allow him easily to accept divine law, and if the moral order
is full of a manifest corruption, it is equally true that to live by
nature's light as Giovanni does is to become the destroyer of life.
Upon this dilemma rests the moral vision of *'Tis Pity She's A
Whore*, and it gives meaning to the title. Annabella is a whore,
but her very human attributes have led her to be one, and in our
pity for her we lament the moral dilemma implicit in the human
condition. 'The gravity of the subject may easily excuse the lightness of the title: otherwise, I had been a severe judge against mine
own guilt,' Ford wrote in his dedicatory epistle to the Earl of
Peterborough, with an obvious pun upon lightness. The title is
more meaningful and more appropriate to the gravity of the
subject than one might immediately suppose.

In man's inability to escape moral uncertainty lies his tragedy.
If he would live in the world he has no alternative but a blind
conformity. If Ford suggests any escape from the problem he
poses it may be in Richardetto's speech to Philotis:

My counsel is that you should free your years
From hazard of these woes, by flying hence
To fair Cremona, there to vow your soul
To holiness a holy votaress,
Leave me to see the end of these extremes.

> All human worldly courses are uneven,
> No life is blessed but the way to heaven.

> (1750–6)

Man may ignore the world and place his hope in the prospect of heaven. If he would live in the world he has no alternative but a blind acceptance of the moral order which runs counter to his highest human attribute, his searching, rational spirit.

IV

If the movement of Ford's tragedies is from an Arcadian setting to a more and more realistic one, *Perkin Warbeck* would appear to be the final stage of his development, for now he casts his moral paradox against the background of his own country and shows it destroying the lives of characters whose actuality the audience cannot doubt. In placing the history of England upon his stage, Ford was following a well-worn dramatic tradition, although one which had been moribund for a quarter of a century;[1] in reviving the history play he wrote with the examples of Marlowe and Shakespeare to guide him. Like them he was interested in the political implications of his story, and *Perkin Warbeck* is an exemplary lesson in the ethics of kingship. Henry VII is set up as a model ruler, with James IV and Perkin Warbeck to emphasize his perfection. What gives this play its particular effect, however, is that the audience is never allowed to embrace the virtue of King Henry with any sense of affirmation; it seems unimportant and unconvincing in the light of Perkin's tragedy.

What is paradoxical about *Perkin Warbeck* is that this most realistic in setting of all Ford's plays is the play in which Ford most effectively questions the very nature of reality. In answer to the ancient question of what makes a king, the play offers the efficient ruler, Henry VII, but it offers also Perkin Warbeck, the impostor with all the outward signs of royalty, who has come himself to believe in his own royalty and who dies a martyr to his own belief. Towards the pretender is directed all of the audience's sympathy, with the loving fidelity of Lady Katherine Gordon to make his tragedy more poignant. The world's justice is triumphant

---

[1] I have treated *Perkin Warbeck* as a history play, stressing its political implications in *The English History Play in the Age of Shakespeare* (Princeton, 1957), pp. 299–305.

at the end, with a restitution of peace and harmony in England, but it has been purchased by the betrayal of Perkin by the Scottish king, and when Perkin goes to the gallows convinced of his own truth the audience is left in a state of doubt and ambivalence. It cannot really choose between the values of Perkin and King Henry; it is unable finally to distinguish appearance from reality.

Perkin Warbeck more than anything else is a play about the impossibility of belief, a motif emphasized in the treachery to his king of Sir William Stanley with which the play opens and repeated in the treachery of Sir Robert Clifford to his friend. Where can one place his faith in a world in which those a man loves most may turn against him? Perkin is a liar, but in his fidelity to his own pretence he attains a glory greater than that of any other in the play. The alternative of truth is exhibited in the sordid role of Lambert Simnel. We leave *Perkin Warbeck* with the feeling that reality may, after all, be only what we think it is, that there is no truth of which man can be certain, and that we may attain some victory by a heroic persistence even in a false pretence. *Perkin Warbeck* cannot answer the questions which it poses. As surely as *'Tis Pity She's A Whore*, it is the tragedy of man's inability to find certainty, to understand reality or to grasp his own position in the universe. This is why *Perkin Warbeck* is entirely characteristic of Ford, and not, as is sometimes argued, something alien to his ordinary dramatic mode. It is a perfect expression of the Caroline scepticism for which Ford stands, the product of a search for moral order which can only resolve itself in paradox, and never in the kind of certainty attained by those Elizabethan forebears whom Ford so assiduously imitated and in whose company he longed in vain to be.

Index

177